National Theatre

ALL ABOUT THEATRE

National Theatre

WALKER BOOKS

AND SUBSIDIARIES

LONDON · BOSTON · SYDNEY · AUCKLAND

The National Theatre would like to
thank the very many people who have
contributed their time, expertise and enthusiasm
to the creation of this book.

Written by Marina McIntyre
Illustrated by RUDE – www.thisisrude.com

Project team for the National Theatre:
Alice King-Farlow, Kate Bone, Emma Gosden, Sarah Corke

Our thanks also to Patrick Harrison, Philippa Milnes-Smith, Alison Rae, Annabel
Thomas, Erin Lee, Nick Cannon, Laura Canter, the children of Jubilee Primary School,
Hackney and the team at Walker Books.

Director of the National Theatre, Rufus Norris
Executive Director, Lisa Burger

This book was inspired by the many extraordinary productions programmed by Nicholas Hytner, Director
of the National Theatre from 2003–2015, and Nick Starr, Executive Director from 2002–2014.
For more information on theatre-making visit us at www.nationaltheatre.org.uk/allabouttheatre

First published 2015 by Walker Books Ltd, 87 Vauxhall Walk, London SE11 5HJ
2 4 6 8 10 9 7 5 3 1
This edition published 2017

DID YOU KNOW?

THEATRE'S NOT JUST ABOUT

ACTING

It's an amazing way to tell stories. Every night people go to the theatre to watch other worlds being created. A play might have been written years ago or devised days before the first performance. Theatre brings people together to experience a story.

But theatre isn't just about what you see on stage. The work begins long before the first night. It takes many different people with many different skills to put on a play. This book tells the story of how we do it at the National Theatre, where everything happens under one roof. We make scenery, costumes, wigs and props. We have departments for lighting, sound, music and video.

You don't need to be the National Theatre to put on a play though. Plays happen everywhere – in schools, village halls and churches, in tents, in old warehouses, even outdoors. The idea of this book is to inspire you to get involved. You could write a play. You could design sets or make costumes. You could be a producer, organizing how a play is put on.

We hope you enjoy discovering some of the ways we make theatre. But most of all we hope you will go and see a play and tell some stories yourself.

Rufus Norris, Director of the National Theatre

CONTENTS

THE MAGIC OF THEATRE

Telling a story through people pretending to be other people dates back thousands of years. In Ancient Greece one or two actors and a chorus performed a play, using only their voices and bodies to create an imaginary world. Today actors wear costumes and carry props, and their performances are often accompanied by elaborate sets and sound and lighting effects. But making theatre has always been about storytelling through speech, movement, space, light and sound. A play must use these to create an illusion for the audience and explore big ideas.

The theatre is magical because it makes the audience forget that what they are watching isn't real. This is called the suspension of disbelief.

Your brain might know that the actor dying on stage in front of you is pretending to die, but the power of the storytelling makes you forget, so that you believe what you are seeing. A good play will always inspire the audience's imagination, taking them far beyond the theatre itself and into other worlds.

And it's not just up to the actors to tell the story. Everything on stage happens for a reason and all kinds of decisions are made behind the scenes before opening night. From what the stage looks like to the music you hear and the kind of costumes the actors wear, it all makes the imaginary world of the play believable, moving and entertaining for the audience.

HOW THIS BOOK WORKS

Making a play is a complicated process. This book will show you how a play is made at the National Theatre, from the first idea to the final curtain. Throughout and in the glossary at the back are interesting theatre words. You will meet different experts and explore different National Theatre productions from the NT's 50-year history and see through them how theatre can be made. There are many other ways to make theatre, though. With clever tricks of the trade and ideas to try at home, you can get involved too.

James Corden in
ONE MAN, TWO GUVNORS

"The National Theatre's building is important, but the human raw material matters most — the administrators, directors, playwrights, actors, stage managers, designers, painters, technicians and musicians."
LAURENCE OLIVIER, 1962

THE ORESTEIA,
a Greek tragedy

A BRIEF HISTORY

People have been putting on plays all around the world for thousands of years. Here are some important moments in the history of Western theatre that influence the way the National Theatre makes plays today.

ANCIENT GREECE Around 500 BC

More than 2,000 years ago the Ancient Greeks came up with the idea of acting. Theatre started as a way of honouring their god Dionysus, but became a way to explore human nature. Some of their types of storytelling are still used today, like comedy (a happy or funny play) and tragedy (a sad play).

SHAKESPEARE AND CO. Around 1599

The Rose and The Curtain were two of the first theatres in London. They were built about ten years before Shakespeare, considered to be the world's greatest playwright, wrote his first play. Theatres could charge entrance fees, so being part of a theatre company became a way to make money and theatres competed to attract audiences. Only men were allowed to act on stage so boys played the female parts. Theatres like the Globe became very popular, but in 1642 the Puritan Parliament closed them all down.

500 BC   1400   1599

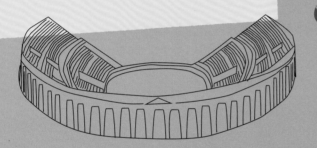

THE NATIVITY,
a Mystery play

MORALITY AND MYSTERY PLAYS Around 1400

Plays in medieval England were based on religious themes. Morality plays were about the struggle between good and evil. Mystery plays told stories from the Bible.

OF THEATRE

COMMEDIA DELL'ARTE
Around 1600

Commedia dell'arte started in Venice and was a form of street theatre. Actors improvised comic scenarios, which meant the action of the play was made up in the moment. All the characters represented certain types of people, like masters, servants, heroes or villains. These 'stock' characters had a specific personality trait, mask, costume and physical gesture that the audience would recognize instantly.

THE MAGISTRATE, a Victorian farce

VICTORIAN THEATRE Around 1881

During Queen Victoria's reign, tickets became cheaper and theatre became even more popular for rich and poor alike. Most theatres in London's West End were built during this time. The first theatre to have electricity powering all its lighting was the Savoy Theatre in London in 1881.

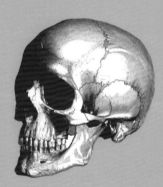

National Theatre

opens on the South Bank

1600 1660 1881 1963 1976

THE RESTORATION
Around 1660

The Restoration era began when King Charles II came to the throne. Theatres were allowed to reopen and women appeared on stage as actors for the first time. Plays from this period were often witty and bawdy, and were popular with wealthy society.

HAMLET, the National Theatre's first production

AFTER THE WARS
Around 1963

During World Wars I and II, theatre helped to raise the country's spirits. But afterwards, cinema and TV became more popular and theatres had to find new ways to attract their audiences. Many theatres, including the National Theatre, were founded to ensure the grand tradition of theatre-making continued. The first National Theatre Company performance was in 1963.

THE NATIONAL THEATRE

Since the time of Queen Victoria people had said that Britain needed a theatre to celebrate the great traditions of British theatre, especially the plays of William Shakespeare. Even so, it took until the 1960s for the first National Theatre production, **Hamlet**, starring Peter O'Toole and directed by Laurence Olivier, to be staged at the Old Vic theatre. In 1976 the National Theatre moved from the Old Vic to its impressive home on the South Bank of the River Thames.

It doesn't stop there. Plays from the National Theatre can move to the West End of London, or tour around the country or even as far away as the USA and Japan. Some plays are filmed and screened live in cinemas around the world by National Theatre Live. But what happens at the National Theatre on a big scale is also going on in theatres up and down the country and around the world. It's the same magic, whether the venue is big or small.

THEATRE TALENT

Some of the most famous actors in the world have performed at the National Theatre. Judi Dench, Ian McKellen, Benedict Cumberbatch, Helen Mirren, Adrian Lester, Michael Gambon, Lenny Henry and Maggie Smith are just a few such names. Hundreds of other talented actors and rising stars have followed in their footsteps. Famous playwrights like Alan Bennett and Tom Stoppard have had their plays premiered (first performed) at the National Theatre.

But theatre is not just about the actors and playwrights. Behind the scenes at the National Theatre is a theatre-making factory. Hundreds of people are hard at work creating props, costumes, wigs, scenery, music and lighting to help bring the actors' performances to life.

STATS & FACTS

In total over 1,000 people work at the National Theatre. Since 1963 the National Theatre has presented more than 900 shows and almost 10,000 actors have been in its productions, playing a total of more than 37,000 roles.

The National Theatre at the Old Vic in 1963 and on the South Bank today

THE OLIVIER

The huge Olivier, named after the famous actor and the National Theatre's first Director, Laurence Olivier, is used for big productions. The stage has a vast revolving section, called the drum revolve, and more than 1,000 people can fit into the auditorium. As in an Ancient Greek amphitheatre, the audience sits in a semi-circle around a circular stage.

THREE THEATRES

The National Theatre has three different theatres, which are different shapes and sizes.

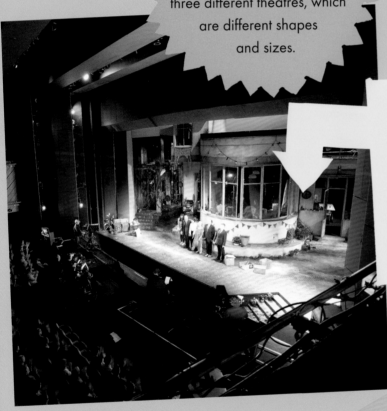

THE LYTTELTON

The Lyttelton has a traditional stage shape, called proscenium arch. The arch frames the action on the stage, like a picture frame. Unlike most proscenium arch theatres, the Lyttelton's arch can be adjusted so the height and width of the stage can change. The auditorium can seat up to 900 people and the seats have excellent views of the stage.

THE DORFMAN

The Dorfman is the smallest and most flexible theatre inside the building, where new exciting and experimental plays can be put on. It can seat up to 450 people, and the seats can be raised, lowered or folded away completely to create different stage spaces.

THE PLAYWRIGHT writes the script for the play. A **composer** might be needed to write original music.

THE DIRECTOR is in charge of what you see on the stage and gets the final say on how everything should look and how it should be performed. The director will choose the cast and then rehearse the play with them. A director might work with a **fight director** for a fight scene, and a **choreographer**, **movement director** or **music director** if there is dancing, singing or live music.

THE DESIGNER comes up with the idea for how everything on the stage should look, including the set, costumes and props, though sometimes there will be a separate **costume designer**.

THE LIGHTING DESIGNER decides on the lighting for the play. The **video designer** designs any video projection. The **lighting operator** works all the lights for each performance.

THE CREATIVE TEAM

WHO'S WHO IN THE THEATRE

It takes many different talents to make and put on a play. Every single member of the creative, acting and production teams has their own role. Theatre is all about working together to make the magic happen.

THE SOUND DESIGNER chooses sound and music for the play, from occasional sound effects to a continuous background soundtrack to set the scene. The **sound operator** works the sound at each performance.

Most plays use most of these people, but each production will have a slightly different team depending on the play.

THE ACTING TEAM

THE STAGE MANAGERS make sure everything runs smoothly during rehearsals and performances. They work backstage, keeping track of the props, making sure actors are where they need to be and giving the **lighting** and **sound operators** their cues.

THE CREW are on hand backstage during the performance to change the scenery. They also reset the stage before every show, making sure the set is ready for the first scene.

THE PRODUCTION TEAM

THE PRODUCTION MANAGER works with the **scenic construction**, **scenic painting** and **props teams** to build the set and make the designer's ideas a reality. They will work with the **lighting**, **sound**, **costume** and **wigs**, **hair and make-up teams**.

THE CAST is made up of the **actors** who will be seen on stage by the audience. Some plays have a cast of just one or two people, while a big musical might have more than 100.

THE PRODUCER is responsible for planning the play, scheduling the performances and managing the budget. In large theatres like the National Theatre there may be lots of different people involved in producing a play. In other theatres one person is the producer.

MAKING A PLAY

The play is chosen

↓

The director and designer discuss their ideas for the play

The actors are cast   The design is agreed

Rehearsals

Props made   Costumes, wigs and make-up made   Lighting and sound designed   The set is built

The fit-up

Technical rehearsals

Dress rehearsal

Preview performances

Opening night

MAKING UP A STORY

Plays tell stories. A playwright's job is to make up a story, in the form of a script, which is not just entertaining to watch, but also explores ideas and makes the audience think about the world differently.

Context

The playwright needs to think of a setting for the play and if it is in the past, present or future. They also need to decide if the story is exploring any historical, social or political ideas or issues.

Themes

The play will have some big ideas or questions which the playwright will keep exploring as the story develops.

A PLAY NEEDS

Characters

The story of the play is told through what the characters say and the way they move around the stage. The audience must believe in every aspect of the characters, from their personalities to their relationships with the other characters.

Plot

A play has to set up a situation and there must be a reason why the story unfolds in the way it doe It should come to an end which i satisfying. Some things should be left to the audience's imagination

Plays take many forms and all of them will use some or all of these components, even if it isn't obvious.

WRITING A SCRIPT

The layout of a script makes it clear who is talking and what is happening on stage.

Stage directions: these describe where the scene takes place or what actions the character is doing. They are often displayed in a different font or style to the dialogue and can be very detailed or simple. Sometimes there are none and it's up to the directors and actors. Enter and Exit mean someone walking on or off the stage.

Characters: the person speaking is labelled so it's clear who says what.

BILL BONES
Grog!!!!

5.- A TERRIBLE ISLAND IN THE BRAIN....

JIM
No grog!!!
No!!!

BONES
Sleep has left me Jim!
Living men will pursue you
But *Ghost* men are the ones who *catch* you!
If I close my eyes, I am *bobbing* off that *terrible* island with Flint upon it.
I am *cold* inside to think of Flint.
Grog-in here-Girl!!!
Holds out his goblet

JIM
I'll get you grog on *one* condition…

BONES
Name it!

JIM
You answer my *questions!*

BONES
Done!

JIM fetches bottle, but keeps it, despite all BONES valiant and ingenious attempts out of his grasp...JIM pours a very small tot BONES drains it off

The script for **TREASURE ISLAND**

Scenes: a play is mad up of scenes. They are like chapters in a book as each scene tells a specific part of the stor making up the whole. A scene is usually set i a particular location.

Dialogue: the words spoken by the characters. A dialogue is two or more people in conversation. If one character speaks their thoughts aloud to the audience, that speech is called a monologue or soliloquy.

Tragedy

Tragedies end sadly, often with one or more people dying. In Ancient Greece, where tragedies were often performed, it was thought that watching these plays could create a feeling called catharsis, which made the audience feel they had been on an emotional journey like the characters.

History

History plays dramatize real events, often the lives of important people, such as kings and queens, or moments of historical importance. Shakespeare wrote several, and they are still written today.

DIFFERENT TYPES OF PLAY

Plays come in many different forms. Here are the most popular.

Comedy

Traditionally any play that ends happily is a comedy, though today we think of comedies as plays that make you laugh. There are lots of different kinds. In **farce** people find themselves in ridiculous, unlikely situations. **Satire** mocks society and people in positions of power, such as politicians, making them look ridiculous.

Drama

A play that is neither a comedy nor a tragedy, but uses some of the elements of both.

Verbatim

In verbatim theatre the playwright uses the recorded voices and speech of real people as the starting point for a play based on a true story.

Immersive

In immersive theatre there is no physical separation between audience and actors, and the audience participate directly in the action of the play. Immersive theatre often happens in spaces that aren't theatres, like warehouses.

Pantomine

Pantomimes are usually based on fairy-tales. Traditionally there is a dame, played by a man, and the leading man is played by a woman.

DIFFERENT TYPES OF THEATRE

Plays can also be performed in different theatrical forms. Here are some of them.

Improvisation

There is no script for an improvised play. The actors and director make up all the elements of the story in the moment of performance, sometimes asking the audience to help.

Devised

There is also no script for a devised play, but instead the actors and director work together to create a story and then perform it for an audience.

Physical

In physical theatre most of the story is told through movement and action rather than dialogue.

Musical

Any play where the story is told partly through song is a musical. Some have music all the way through and some have a few musical numbers mixed in with normal spoken scenes.

**...ianne Elliott
DIRECTOR**

In a book you can stop to ponder and reflect. You absolutely can't do that in the theatre. There's a huge risk in adapting something that is well-known and well-loved, because people come with ideas of how the play should be.

**Anna Maxwell Martin
ACTOR**

It felt really special to be part of a landmark production like **His Dark Materials** – with those bears, the puppets. Nicholas Hytner, the director, created something beautiful. The audience were silent all the way through. People thought I was a twelve-year-old girl. That's the magic of theatre: the audience believe what they are being shown.

USING A STORY

Sometimes, rather than making up a story of their own, a playwright can adapt a story that exists in another form. Adaptations can be based on many different sources, from books and films to songs and diaries or even another play.

RETELLING A STORY

Adapting a story for the stage is a challenge. The playwright does not have to create the plot, characters and themes from scratch, but does have to make those elements work on stage. If the story being adapted is well known to the audience, they will have expectations about what the play will be like. A playwright has to try and tell the story in a new and different way. To do this they might cut out parts of the plot or certain characters or change the context of the play.

OLD TO NEW

Sometimes a playwright will use an existing play's story and do something different with it. Ancient Greek tragedies, like **Medea** or **Oedipus Rex**, are often translated so modern audiences can enjoy them. Shakespeare wrote 37 plays during his lifetime. Playwrights often edit his scripts, cutting and adapting them to make them more relevant to a modern audience. They might also rewrite the story completely. For example, a playwright might rewrite **Romeo and Juliet** as if the story was happening today, using modern dialogue instead of Shakespeare's words.

Playwrights can also use an existing play as the basis for their own story. **Rosencrantz and Guildenstern are Dead** by Tom Stoppard is based around two minor characters in **Hamlet**. It uses events and characters from Shakespeare's play, but presents them in a new way, making the audience think differently about events in the original play.

THEATRE WORDS

A **WRIGHT** is the old word for a person who makes something. A shipwright builds ships and a playwright builds stories.

PAGE AND SCREEN

Many plays are adapted from books. Books are many thousands of words long, but plays have to be much shorter, to tell the story in two or three hours. The playwright therefore has to choose the characters and parts of the plot that have the most dramatic potential. Books also allow the reader inside the heads of the different characters. They make it very easy to understand each character's motives and they can tell the reader what the characters are thinking and feeling. A playwright has to write dialogue that makes the audience emotionally connect with the characters in the same way. Films can also be successfully adapted into plays, although staging some of the action live can be challenging.

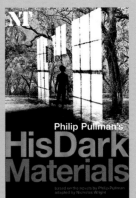

Philip Pullman's
His Dark Materials
based on the novels by Philip Pullman
adapted by Nicholas Wright

2003
Based on the novels by Philip Pullman
Adapted by Nicholas Wright
Director Nicholas Hytner
Set Designer Giles Cadle
Costume Designer Jon Morrell

Nicholas Wright adapted Philip Pullman's trilogy of books, **His Dark Materials**, into one play in two parts for the National Theatre. The story moves through parallel universes and there are strange creatures like daemons and armoured bears. Nicholas Wright had to shorten the plot, cut some of the characters and also think about how to move between different times and places successfully in the script.

HIS DARK MATERIALS

MEET THE WRITERS

Ben Power
PLAYWRIGHT

Adapting a play is about finding an answer to the question, 'why tell this story now?' I'm always inspired by the challenge of making an old play, or a play in another language, or a film or novel speak as a piece of theatre directly to an audience today. It's all about collaboration, though, and a script isn't finished until it's benefitted from the input of everyone involved. The script of one of my plays usually changes right up to opening night! Making **Medea**, a very old play, relevant to a modern audience was one of the most challenging and exciting new productions I've done.

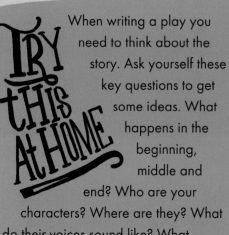

When writing a play you need to think about the story. Ask yourself these key questions to get some ideas. What happens in the beginning, middle and end? Who are your characters? Where are they? What do their voices sound like? What emotions are they experiencing?

Michaela Coel
PLAYWRIGHT

At drama school I decided that I would write a one-woman play. I just started writing based on memories from my secondary school. It was inspired by the people I grew up with, the area, the buses, the journeys through London. I had gaps between classes, so I had every day to write and write and write. Before I knew it, I had a play of an hour and a half called **Chewing Gum Dreams**! There was a theatre called The Yard, which was accepting submissions. I sent in my play and heard nothing back. When I finally met with the director he said, 'This is great, but take out the ending, she doesn't die. Change it.' So I changed it. It was very helpful. I built the set. The Yard lent me loads of materials. I would stand on the street handing out fliers, I did all the marketing. The show sold really well.

Bryony Lavery
PLAYWRIGHT

If I am adapting a book into a play I read and re-read, because books continue to present new sides of themselves. The benefit of adapting is that I learn a huge amount about structure, plot, character and dialogue from having to immerse myself in the brain of another writer. When I finally think I know what the heart of the idea is, I start. At first I try and use as much of the dialogue and authorial voice as possible. Eventually, I take a mighty leap and make it my own.

Lucy Prebble
PLAYWRIGHT

Look for areas and subject matter which fascinate you. Look for worlds that are unexplored. You can do enough research to write about anything you want. You don't have to be a scientist to write about science. You just have to be a writer. Never feel intimidated.

ONE MAN, TWO GUVNORS

One Man, Two Guvnors
by Richard Bean
based on *The Servant of Two Masters* by Carlo Goldoni

...d Bean, based on **The Servant of**
...sters by Carlo Goldoni, with songs by
...ding
...Nicholas Hytner
...Comedy Director Cal McCrystal
...Mark Thompson

The National Theatre's slapstick comedy **One Man, Two Guvnors** was an adaptation of an existing story. The writer Richard Bean adapted the play from **The Servant of Two Masters**, a 1743 Italian commedia dell'arte play by the playwright Carlo Goldoni.

The original play was set in Florence, but Richard Bean moved the action to Brighton in 1963. His characters have different names, but other than that, all the elements of the adaptation were true to the original. The actors improvised, interacted with the audience and had running jokes and comic set pieces. In one hilarious scene an audience member had to help Francis, played by James Corden, move a trunk.

Nadia Fall DIRECTOR

As soon as I have read a play, I have an instinctive response to the story and relate to a part of it – whether it's a character or a scene. You always bring yourself to a play you are directing. You ask what it is about – marriage, justice, something else. If a play is set in a certain period, you look at what was going on in the world at that time, and how that feeds the story. If it's more timeless, you find what you think will make the story come most alive.

PICKING A PLAY

Theatres choose plays for all kinds of reasons, but always have to balance creative ideas with practical questions about budgets or dates. Some theatres always put on one sort of play, for example just new plays. Some present plays that are produced in other theatres and are on tour. But most theatres will aim to programme a variety of plays to appeal to lots of different audiences.

The National Theatre puts on more than twenty plays every year so it can make a very wide choice of plays, including comedy, tragedy, new plays and classics, plays by Shakespeare and plays from around the world. Ideas for plays come from the theatre and from directors and writers. They might suggest an adaptation of a book or a new idea for staging a well-known play. The theatre looks for plays that have been forgotten or neglected, which an audience might enjoy discovering, and for new voices and stories not heard before on stage. Plays can be written and staged quickly, to respond to something going on in the world.

The National Theatre can have 60–70 new plays at different stages of development, including plays that have been commissioned from writers and plays in development in the Studio.

WORKSHOPS

Workshops are a way for playwrights, directors, actors and designers to experiment with different ideas and discover what works before a play is chosen. They take place before rehearsals begin. Workshops are particularly useful for new plays and ones that might be difficult to stage. Different actors might be in the workshops and the final play.

STUDIO

At the National Theatre, workshops are held in the Studio. It is an exciting place for experimentation. Playwrights hear their words spoken by actors for the first time and directors develop interesting new ideas. Plays can go through long periods of time in the Studio before they are performed at the National Theatre (**War Horse** had several workshops over two years) and not everything tried in the Studio will actually be staged.

Rory Kinnear
ACTOR

At the Studio you're entering a project on the ground level. Nothing might come of it, but to feel part of the creative process at such an early stage, to witness the moment where a writer is hearing his words collide with an actor's voice for the first time is wonderfully invigorating.

A TREASURE ISLAND workshop at the National Theatre Studio

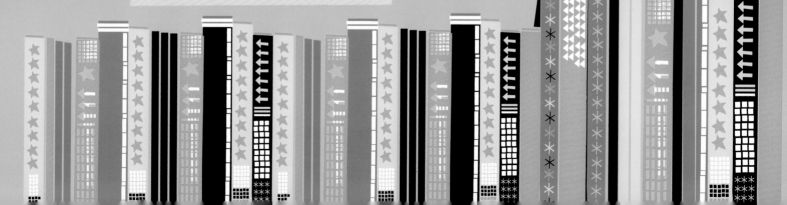

THE VISION

When the play has been chosen the director will work with the designer and other members of the creative team, like a choreographer or a video designer, to decide exactly how the story will be told on stage. Their vision will apply to all aspects of the play's staging, from the look of the set to the way the music sounds. If the director is staging a new play, these decisions are made for the first time and might involve the playwright. If it is a new production of an existing play, the director and the designer have to decide how they want to stage their own version.

Often the director and the designer will have some big ideas that they will decide on. The director might decide to have an all-female cast or have all the different roles played by only three actors. The designer might have an idea for the staging, like video projection, which will influence the way the set is designed. Or it could involve choreography (planned sequences of movement) at a certain point in the action. It might also include using puppets to tell the story.

WAR HORSE

2007
Based on a novel by Michael Morpurgo
Adapted by Nick Stafford
In association with Handspring Puppet Company
Directors Marianne Elliott and Tom Morris
Designer/Drawings Rae Smith

**Tim Hatley
DESIGNER**

There are many, many ways of staging a play. There's never a right way or a wrong way, or a set way. A director will expect a designer to understand what they're saying, and turn that into three dimensions.

PRODUCTIONS

A play can be staged in many different ways. A director and creative team will bring their imaginations and ideas to a play, even one that has been staged many thousands of times, to create their own new production. This will be a new interpretation of the play and present the themes and characters in new ways. For example the director might decide to move the play's story to a different time or place to the original.

War Horse is about a boy, Albert, who enlists in the army during the First World War and risks his life to find his horse, Joey. The directors, Marianne Elliott and Tom Morris, worked with the designer, Rae Smith, on the vision. Here, Marianne Elliott describes what they wanted to achieve:

"Often you start with absolutely no idea of how to stage or direct a play, but the most important thing is to have an emotional connection to the material. Then everything else will follow. Using puppets for the horses was the first idea. Then for the set Rae came up with the idea that Captain Nicholls, a major character who is killed early on, has a sketchbook. The back wall of the stage became a ripped piece from his sketchbook and we used video projection to change the sketches from romantic rural drawings to black-and-white drawings of hell in the trenches."

2012
Based on the novel by Mark Haddon
Adapted by Simon Stephens
Directed by Marianne Elliott
Designed by Bunny Christie

MEET THE DIRECTOR

The director has to decide how best to tell the play's story to the audience.

Marianne Elliott directed **The Curious Incident of the Dog in the Night-Time**, a mystery story about Christopher, who is talented at maths and fascinated by prime numbers, but finds it hard to understand other people. The book the play is adapted from is told from Christopher's perspective, so Marianne Elliott and the designer Bunny Christie had to find a way to let the audience see inside his mind. Here, Marianne Elliott describes reading the script for the first time:

❝ As a director you have to understand what the original writer was aiming for. I realized Mark Haddon was trying to get the reader to be Christopher. So in our adaptation, we tried to get the audience to see things through Christopher's eyes. That was a massive challenge. There was a huge amount of work that started way before we got into rehearsals: conversations with the writer, conversations with the designer, a workshop in the National Theatre Studio with some actors, conversations with the rest of the creative team including the choreographers. We're talking months. Then Bunny Christie and I went away and shut ourselves in a room for a couple of weeks and storyboarded by drawing pictures of each scene to show how one turns into another. The script was a blank sheet of dialogue, with no stage directions. That's how Simon Stephens writes. So we filled in all the gaps. By the time we went into rehearsals we knew exactly what we were going to do.

We realized the set should be a magic box, like Christopher's brain. We wanted the set to show him working out maths problems. It became clear that we wanted a very fluid space that could change from one scene and location to another very quickly. So we decided to use video projections, and the video designer, Finn Ross, was in on the design process before we went into rehearsal. ❞

"MY NAME IS CHRISTOPHER JOHN FRANCIS BOONE. I KNOW ALL THE COUNTRIES OF THE WORLD AND THE CAPITAL CITIES. AND EVERY PRIME NUMBER UP TO 7,507."

The original cast rehearse the movement for THE CURIOUS INCIDENT OF THE DOG IN THE NIGHT-TIME

Finn Ross
VIDEO DESIGNER

Video projection in the West End show

We use video materials, like projection, TV and LED. It's a very direct line of communication to the audience. In **The Curious Incident of the Dog in the Night-Time**, the intention was to celebrate Christopher's unique perspective and to help the audience understand his difficulties in coping. We used video as the texture of the inside of his mind. It also helps show where we are: it can transform a place instantly. We found a graphic language through which we could quickly transport ourselves between multiple locations, for instance when Christopher is navigating London and the Tube.

Ben Thompson
PUPPETEER

There are moments when it's as if the puppet has done something without you making it do it. The movements become unconscious and instinctive and it's these moments that make the audience believe. They know in their head the puppet is not real, but their eyes and their heart tell them it is.

PUPPETS

Sometimes plays will need puppets and puppeteers to tell the story. An idea like this is so central to the director's vision it is decided on right at the very start of the play-making process. Directors and designers will often use puppets to bring animals or strange creatures to life, like in **War Horse** or **His Dark Materials** at the National Theatre.

MAKING A PUPPET MOVE

Making the way a puppet moves and interacts on stage look convincing is a complicated process that takes lots of research and practice. Puppeteers have to think about all these things:

STILLNESS

Movement is how a puppet conveys emotion and thought, but it's in moments of stillness that the audience can process what they have seen. A puppeteer won't make the puppet move all the time, but will leave little pauses. But the puppet will always breathe.

BREATH

The audience need to believe the puppet is alive and seeing it breathe is a great way to achieve this. It can be as simple as gently moving the puppet's ribcage.

RHYTHM

Puppets that move in a repetitive way can look robotic. Changing the rhythm with which they walk or react is a good way of making their movements look more natural as well as showing their emotional state.

WEIGHT

Puppets can levitate, karate chop in the air or fly like superheroes, but they have to obey the same law of gravity as we do if an audience are to believe in them. So if they jump, they need to bend their legs first, rather than just floating up into the air.

WAR HORSE

2007
Based on a novel by Michael Morpurgo
Adapted by Nick Stafford
In association with Handspring Puppet Company
Directors Marianne Elliott and Tom Morris
Designer/Drawings Rae Smith

Toby Olié PUPPETEER

In **War Horse** the puppets, designed by South Africa's Handspring Puppet Company, were made out of aluminium, cane, gauze and bicycle brake cables. The puppeteers moved the puppets and made all the animal noises. Here, original cast member Toby Olié describes it:

I was always making puppets when I was little. I would make a shoebox version of whatever I'd seen at the theatre. So when I was studying puppetry at university and was asked about being involved in **War Horse**, I jumped at the chance. At first Joey, the horse, was made for two puppeteers – one person on the front legs and one on the back. However, we ended up with three puppeteers, as we quickly realized that the head and ears have to be animated at all times, to enable the horse to express itself. I puppeteered the back legs at first, and then moved on to operate the head. Initially we did a lot of research into how horses behave. We visited horses in military stables to see the differences between them and farm horses, because Joey goes through that journey. We also spent a long time perfecting the puppet's walk, trot and gallop, as well as how it could carry a rider. Then, when we felt happy with that, we started working with actors in the context of the show. You begin to put yourself in the mindset of a horse. When you are playing Joey, you don't listen to the spoken dialogue, but you react to the pitch and emotional tone of it.

THE CAST

Wendy Spon
HEAD OF CASTING

We're a resource of knowledge about actors and their work. A director will come to us and talk about their ideas. Then we set about making lists for each role and investigating who is available, talking to agents, and whittling it down to the right number of people for the director to see at audition. People imagine directors just work with people they already know, which is not true at all. They rely on us to introduce them to people they don't know. A cast will be a mixture of people directors have worked with before, people they have always been interested in working with, and people we introduce them to. If you're thinking of being a casting director, you'll have to go to the theatre at least three times a week for the rest of your life. I go to the theatre all the time. That's the only way. It's not just about having an opinion, it's about having an informed opinion. You have to put your own favourites to one side and absorb what it is the director wants. It's about understanding them as well as the actor, I suppose.

THE PEOPLE FOR THE PLAY

Once the director knows how the play is going to be staged, they can start to think about the actors they need for the play. The casting director and agents suggest people and then the director holds auditions.

CAREFUL CASTING

Casting directors are experts on actors. Their job is to help directors find the right people for the parts in a play. They have an encyclopedic knowledge of actors and their different abilities. The casting director will chat with the director about the kind of actors they need and come up with a list of possibilities. Some directors want a long list, maybe even up to 30 or 40, while others might only want three or four.

ACTING AGENTS

Most professional actors have an agent who represents them. Agents suggest actors to directors or casting directors and arrange for them to attend auditions. If a casting director asks for a particular actor who is busy, an agent might suggest another actor. Actors often work in television and film as well as theatre, so might well be working on another project.

WHAT FITS THE PART

What a director is looking for depends a lot on the play. They might be looking for an actor who can sing, dance or play a musical instrument. They might need an actor who can speak French or do an excellent regional accent. If the play is by Shakespeare, they will want an actor who is confident in speaking in verse. If it's a devised piece of theatre, they will want an actor who is excellent at improvisation. Ultimately though, a director will want an actor who they feel instinctively understands and connects with the part. This is what they will be looking for in auditions.

AUDITIONS

Auditions work in lots of different ways. Usually directors want to see actors perform part of the play. Sometimes the director will select a piece for the actors to prepare in advance or just ask the actors to choose part of the play they like. Sometimes actors will have never seen the piece before the audition and will only be given a couple of minutes to read it through before they have to perform it. Some directors prefer to hold workshop auditions, where lots of actors work on a scene together. That gives the director a chance to see how the actors interact with each other and behave as a group, not just one by one. If there is a lot of singing or dancing in the play, or it is a musical, the actor might have to have an extra audition with a music director.

During an audition a director is thinking about what it will be like to work with an actor. Does the actor understand their vision? After the actor has performed their piece, the director might ask them to try doing it differently. The director will want to see if the actor can listen and understand the direction. The director might still be trying out new ideas, so the more adaptable the actor the better.

Not all actors will have to audition. When a theatre puts on a play like **Hamlet** the director will have decided who will be playing Hamlet because it's such a key role.

Arthur Darvill with his TREASURE ISLAND script

tricks of the trade

TIPS FOR ACTORS

❋ Make sure you are prepared. Read the play and think about your character's role in it.

❋ Some actors like to learn the script in advance, but you don't always need to do this. It's more important to listen and respond to what the director wants.

❋ If you are asked to try doing something differently, listen carefully. It doesn't mean you are getting it wrong. The director just wants to see how adaptable you are.

❋ Don't take it personally if you don't get the part.

❋ Believe in yourself. Don't put yourself down. Auditions are nerve-racking for everyone. Remember, the director will want you to do well.

BELIEVE IN YOURSELF

AUDITIONING

Paterson Joseph ACTOR

Olivia Vinall ACTOR

Paterson Joseph in THE RECRUITING OFFICER

Years ago I was auditioning for a musical and I had prepared a sad opera song about a young man being sent off to be a soldier, 'Non più andrai' from **The Marriage of Figaro**. But I hadn't prepared any movements – I was just going to stand by the piano and sing it. When I got there I suddenly thought: 'I've got to do some acting.' I didn't really know what all the words meant. And I just started skipping and dancing around the stage, singing, trying to look animated. There was a big silence afterwards. I think they were just shocked by what they had seen. I wanted to die. I didn't get that job, needless to say.

I'm nervous every time I audition, but I think that's just me – I'm nervous every time I go on stage! If I'm not feeling nervous I get a little bit worried. Having that adrenaline can help you.

I think learning the lines before an audition is so important. Sometimes you can try to convince yourself that it'll be fine with the script, but it really does free you up. You can really listen to the other person, and you are less stuck – you can wave your hands around. With Shakespeare, make sure it makes sense to you. If you don't understand it, you can't make anyone else understand it.

Olivia Vinall in OTHELLO

Arthur Darvill
ACTOR

Bijan Sheibani
DIRECTOR

Auditions are the strangest thing in the world. You never know how they are going to go. The ones that have gone badly have been when I hadn't had time to prepare enough, but thought I had. I've had to learn a speech – you find that happens particularly for Shakespeare plays. I did two auditions where I blanked and forgot my lines and grabbed a script. Then I became nervous it would keep happening. There is only so much you can control and so much that you can't. You don't know how people in the room are feeling that day, what mood they are in. The best auditions feel like a rehearsal and that you're working together with the director. The worst are where you feel judged. If there is time I try and learn the lines of the speech. Read it as much as you can. Get a feeling of the character. Give the director something that is surprising. I once had really good advice from another actor: give them something they haven't seen. Always try something different.

In my auditions I will begin by talking to the actor about their previous work in order to get to know them a little bit. I might then describe the play, and how I intend to work on it. Finally I will ask the actor to read a section of the play, and we will discuss it in some detail. This will allow me and the actor to see what it might be like to rehearse together. It might also give me a sense of what they will do in the final production, though I'm not usually looking for a finished performance. I might also be looking to see how flexible the actor is, so I might ask them to try reading the part in a different way. Usually it feels clear when you have found the right actor. Sometimes auditions can surprise you. You learn a lot about the play, and sometimes you change your mind about what kind of actor you're looking for.

I DID MY BEST

tricks of the trade

TIPS FOR DIRECTORS

❋ Try to put the actors at their ease. If you don't, you may never find out what they are capable of. Every actor should leave the audition feeling they did their best, whether or not they get the job.

❋ When you are giving direction, try to be as clear as possible. Don't focus on the negatives, just focus on what you want.

❋ Try acting. It will help you understand your actors better.

Arthur Darvill in
TREASURE ISLAND

CHOREOGRAPHY

VOICE

FACIAL EXPRESSION

ReH

BLOCKING

GESTURE

REHEARSALS

Actors are **OFF-BOOK** when they have learned their lines, as they are no longer having to look at the book, or script. Some directors want this by the first week of rehearsals, while others will let the actors read from the script for longer. All directors will want actors to have learned their lines by the time they are running through the play.

PRACTICE MAKES PERFECT

In rehearsals actors become familiar with their parts, the other actors and also the play as a whole. Directors all have different ways of rehearsing, but will want to help the actors find ways to make their characters and the story believable.

REHEARSING IT RIGHT

During rehearsals the director will want the actors to feel relaxed and not self-conscious about pretending to be someone else. Some start with games, exercises or yoga to help the actors warm up physically. Others will sit down with the actors, discuss the play's big ideas and analyse every moment, gradually working towards acting it out.

By the end of the rehearsal period actors will have spent time on each scene, and probably have run through the whole play several times. The amount of rehearsal time depends on the theatre and the type of play. The National Theatre usually rehearses plays for six weeks or more, including the technical rehearsals in the theatre.

READ-THROUGHS

These are when all the actors read through the whole play together. It helps give the company a sense of the play before they break it down into scenes to rehearse.

RUN-THROUGHS

The director will rehearse every scene at least once before the actors can start running through whole acts (groups of scenes) at a time, and then the whole play. Actors will be off-book and thinking about their character's journey through the play.

TECHNICAL REHEARSALS (The 'Tech')

The tech is when the actors move from the rehearsal room into the theatre. The acting and the technical effects, such as lighting and sound, are rehearsed together, usually the week before performances start.

DRESS REHEARSALS

These are run-throughs in full costume with all the technical elements. They are meant to be like a performance, just without an audience. A director won't usually stop a dress rehearsal.

James Corden and Oliver Chris rehearsing ONE MAN, TWO GUVNORS

EMIL AND THE DETECTIVES

National Theatre

EMIL AND THE DETECTIVES

by Erich Kästner
adapted by Carl Miller

2013
By Erich Kästner
Adapted by Carl Miller
Directed by Bijan Sheibani
Designed by Bunny Christie

Here, director Bijan Sheibani describes rehearsals for the National Theatre's production of the adventure story **Emil and the Detectives**:

We began with a workshop, as we had lots of questions. How can we have Emil jumping from a moving train? How can we create a chase through the sewers? We tried lots of different ideas and began to find a theatrical language for the production. We also had to find lots of children. The casting department went to drama groups, children's acting agencies, and we also involved several schools. Eventually we had 180 children in the play. In each performance there were 50 children in the chorus and ten principal children.

We had two weeks rehearsing with just the principal children. We explored what life was like in Berlin in 1929, and we began to do lots of work on the text. The adult company joined after two weeks and they were responsible for creating the atmospheres of each place, such as Emil's village or the streets of Berlin. There was lots and lots of movement work because Berlin was a very busy city. We watched films of the time and noticed how machine-like the city was, so we wanted to create a very choreographed and orderly city that was confusing, overwhelming and exciting for Emil, a boy from the countryside.

Anne-Marie Duff
ACTOR

HOW TO ACT

Actors use their voices and bodies to tell the play's story. Different plays require different styles of acting and for each part an actor will find a way to make their portrayal of their character as convincing and as truthful as possible.

If it's a period piece I get into character by using historical accounts. I'll also think about the music or fashions from that time. With modern pieces or plays set in abstract times you create a shared world with the cast. Directors have their own techniques for developing characterizations. Some encourage sharing details of the characters' lives or improvising past events. I always go through the script and make lists. What do other characters say about me and are they speaking the truth? What do I say about myself and am I telling the truth?

Jeannette Nelson
HEAD OF VOICE

I make sure the audience can hear the actors. They have to be loud, but sound like real people. Warming up is extremely important and I spend fifteen to twenty minutes on a vocal warm-up. There might be a physical warm-up as well. The actors have to prepare their breathing muscles and the muscles of their mouth and tongue. Acting on a big stage is a very strenuous physical activity.

THINKING IT THROUGH

Actors should make their characters real. If they don't believe in their character, no one in the audience will. During rehearsals, actors must think about:

THE SCRIPT The script contains lots of clues about each character. Actors will read the play many times and make sure they understand every single line.

THE OTHER CHARACTERS
Actors will think about how their character reacts and responds to the other characters in the play. They will think about how their words fit into the bigger whole of the play and tell the story.

THEIR CHARACTER
Actors use their imagination to develop their character. They will think about how the character feels and what motivates their actions throughout the play.

THE WORLD OF THE PLAY
Actors will research the world the playwright has created and think about the different ideas and issues the play is exploring.

METHOD ACTING

Some actors use a technique called method acting to get themselves into character. The idea came from a Russian director called Constantin Stanislavski in the early 20th century, who believed that actors should make their performances as realistic as possible by living the lives of their characters. Actors should use their own experiences of emotion to inspire their performances. Some actors find their character stays with them even when they are not on stage or in rehearsal.

VOICE AND BODY

Actors also have to think about how they will use their voice and body to express the character's personality, thoughts and feelings.

KNOW YOUR DIALECT

An accent or dialect can be a very important part of a character, and a way for the actor to show the audience when and where a play is set.

KNOW YOUR FACE

Actors use their eyes and mouths to create different facial expressions.

KNOW YOUR VOLUME

An actor's voice is an incredibly important tool. Even if an actor is whispering, the people sitting furthest away from the stage must be able to hear what is being said. Actors learn to project their voices so the audience can hear them without them having to shout. A voice coach helps them use all their muscles to breathe in a way that makes their lungs fill with as much air as possible.

KNOW YOUR SOUND

To make their performance convincing and expressive, actors will vary the tone, intonation and pitch of what they say and their diction (the way they pronounce words). They also need to consider the pace at which they say their lines. What words will they emphasize and when will they pause?

KNOW YOUR BODY

Actors think about every part of their body, from the position of their hands to the way they walk around the stage.

Benedict Cumberbatch and Naomie Harris in FRANKENSTEIN

tricks of the trade

All actors warm up before they go on stage. These are some of the ways they do it.

❋ Reach up high, then flop over at the waist so your arms dangle to the floor, breathe in and out, then, very slowly, stand up straight.

❋ Have a good yawn to stretch your throat, then hum for several minutes.

These tongue-twisters are great for warming up the voice. Try repeating:
The sixth sick sheikh's sixth sheep's sick.
Many an anemone sees an enemy anemone.
Red lorry, yellow lorry.

STAGECRAFT

During rehearsals, actors will need to explore how to move around the stage and perform as a group, which is also called an ensemble.

GESTURE

Actors should think about how they will move their arms and hands. Gesturing too little can make a performance seem lifeless and wooden. Gesturing too much can seem forced and over the top. Actors need to find gestures that feel, and therefore look, natural, but can be easily seen at a distance from the stage.

Gesture

AREAS OF A STAGE

Each area of the stage has a different name. When 'blocking' a scene, a director tells the actor which part of the stage they would like them to move to. The stage position always relates to the actor. Stage right will be on the actor's right as they face the audience.

UPSTAGE RIGHT	UPSTAGE CENTRE	UPSTAGE LEFT
STAGE RIGHT	STAGE CENTRE	STAGE LEFT
DOWNSTAGE RIGHT	DOWNSTAGE CENTRE	DOWNSTAGE LEFT

AUDIENCE

BLOCKING

Blocking is when the director works with the actor to decide how the actor will stand, sit or move around the stage for each of their lines. It sounds simple, but deciding on an actor's physical position on stage is a very important part of the rehearsal process. Without it, actors might end up standing in front of each other, walking into each other or obscuring the audience's view of the stage. Actors often imagine the stage has a 'fourth wall', which means they can act as though the audience aren't there. Talking directly to the audience from the stage is known as 'breaking the fourth wall'.

Blocking

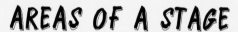

MOVEMENT DIRECTION

Movement can be an essential part of telling the play's story and a movement director works with the director and actors to develop the play's physical language. Movement directors help actors with anything from individual gestures to how to move as a group around the stage or how to perform complicated lifts into the air.

CHOREOGRAPHY AND DANCE

If the production has lots of singing and dancing (as in a piece of musical theatre) or the characters have to dance as a part of the scene, a choreographer will create those dances. Some productions might also include dances that reflect the historical period or social context of a play, like jive in the 1960s or a jig in an Elizabethan play.

Choreography

TAKING DIRECTION

An actor will ensure the way they have imagined and interpreted their character not only feels real, but fits with the director's vision for the play. Actors spend a lot of time thinking about their characters and will have lots of good ideas. But the director always has the final say and the actor must respect their decision.

If a director wants something done differently, sometimes they will show actors how and where they want them to stand. They might also read a line to show the actor how they want it said, which is called a line reading. Some directors will talk through the different options with the actors, but let them come to their own decisions.

Imogen Knight
MOVEMENT DIRECTOR

I consider myself both a movement director and a choreographer. Both are about creating a physical language. I often work with people who have had little or no movement experience. It's one of the best parts of the job, because the work they create is raw and based on instinct. I love learning how someone moves. My favourite projects are when the physical work is central and has a strong presence from the first day of rehearsals until the final performance.

GIVING NOTES

During a run-through, the director will not interrupt (unless something has gone seriously wrong). Instead, they will keep notes and go through them with the actors afterwards. Some notes are for the whole cast and others are for individual actors. The director may deliver these to the actor in private.

STAGE SKILLS

Sometimes actors might need to learn some special skills to help them develop their stagecraft. Making sure every detail is as perfect as possible will make the play seem real for them and the audience.

STAGE FIGHTING

For hundreds of years plays have involved actors fighting with weapons, like swords and knives, or with their bare hands. Fights can be the most dramatic moments in a play, and it's the job of the fight director to ensure that they look as realistic as possible, but nobody gets hurt. Fighting is a form of physical storytelling, so as well as planning all the moves and making sure the actors' timings are just right, the fight director will encourage the actors to think about how they can express their emotions through their actions.

Stage fighting is like dancing, in that it's all choreographed. The only difference is that it's got to look as real as it can without being real. The fights I direct range from a sword fight to a mass brawl to a simple push or slap. The important thing is that the fight is part of the story, and makes sense within the world of the play. Obviously you can't actually hit or kick someone, because you would hurt them. I divert the audience's attention and then the next thing they hear is the sound of the blow, or the reaction. It's all about the actors practising. The fight in the last act of **Hamlet** is one of my favourites. It's one of the best-written fights ever. It was an amazing experience to do that on the Olivier stage.

Fighting in
HAMLET

THEATRE WORDS

KNAPS are the noises actors make to create the sound of a slap or punch. It's normally someone clapping or slapping their own chest or leg. The timing is crucial for it to look and sound convincing.

Timing it right in
ONE MAN, TWO GUVNORS

Goose puppet in WAR HORSE

COMIC TIMING

If an actor is playing a comic part, the director and movement director will help them with their timings, to make sure they get the biggest possible laugh from the audience. It's important for an actor to deliver a line in just the right way, pausing so the audience know a joke is coming. The same is true for more physical slapstick comedy. Comic movement is often about repetition and exaggeration. Actors need to fall over at just the right moment for the scene to seem convincing, which takes a lot of practice.

CRYING ON CUE

Sometimes there will be a moment in a play when an actor needs to cry real tears. Actors have lots of different techniques for making their crying look convincing. Some will try and completely immerse themselves in that particular moment of the play, so their tears become a natural reaction to the character's situation. Others might think about something sad that has happened to them or imagine a situation that makes them upset.

PUPPETS

If puppets are being used in the production the actors will need to practise with them in rehearsals. They need to animate the puppets and learn how to interact with them on stage. If a puppeteer is operating a puppet, like the wheeled goose in **War Horse**, they will need to practise making the puppet's movements expressive.

Often in rehearsals the actors won't have the finished puppets to work with, but instead will improvise with the materials they have available. In **War Horse**, the process for developing the horse puppets began with cardboard horse heads, then a ladder being carried by two actors to represent the horses' spines. Finally, prototypes for the finished puppets were made from metal, cane and gauze and these were used in rehearsals.

47

ACTING SHAKESPEARE

Shakespeare's plays are filled with great stories and big ideas. Acting in a Shakespeare play can be incredibly exhilarating, but also a challenge. At first the language can seem difficult, and there is also a history of different interpretations by famous actors, so there can be a lot to live up to. But playing one of Shakespeare's most famous roles can be the highlight of an actor's career. Here, two actors describe what Shakespeare means to them:

OLIVIA VINALL

"I remember being given the 'Double, double toil and trouble' speech from **Macbeth** to learn at school. I had no idea what some of those words meant, but I came up with images for them in my head, and that felt very exciting. There's something really magical about Shakespeare. It feels timeless, because we're all still struggling with these things in our lives – jealousy, and love, and abandonment. I've always loved seeing different productions. There's something about **Hamlet** that means you want to see it more than once. Nothing feels quite as open and endless as Shakespeare for me. That's why I always go back to it. My favourite character might just be Rosalind in **As You Like It**, because she is clever and witty, and the way she expresses herself feels really truthful. I love her bravery. She's not in any way a drip. I love that."

Olivia Vinall and
Adrian Lester in OTHELLO

Lenny Henry in
THE COMEDY OF ERRORS

MEET THE ACTORS

LENNY HENRY

"I was never into Shakespeare at school. I was working class with Jamaican parents – what did Shakespeare have to do with me? Then later I took an Open University English Literature degree and studied a module of Shakespeare every term – sometimes **Othello**, sometimes **Twelfth Night** – and my penultimate year was a Shakespeare jamboree, a whole year of him! I was dreaming in iambic pentameter (the rhythm Shakespeare wrote his verse in) and finally I gave in: I was beginning to 'get' it. The stories were for everyone, they featured universal themes of love, loss, mourning, betrayal, revenge, pride, hubris, envy; things that everyone can understand whether they're upper, middle or lower class or whether they're from London, Jamaica or Dubrovnik. I now appreciate Shakespeare because his language affects me: his lyrical choice is extraordinary, his situations priceless, his humour delicious. Shakespeare is for all of us – toffs, stiffs and scruffs. Everyone."

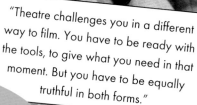

Anna Maxwell Martin
STAGE AND SCREEN

"Theatre challenges you in a different way to film. You have to be ready with the tools, to give what you need in that moment. But you have to be equally truthful in both forms."

Julie Walters
STORYTELLING

"There's nothing that's as exciting as theatre, because your performance is there and then in that moment with that audience: it's what actors are about, really. You're telling the story."

Simon Russell Beale
LEARNING LINES

"I try to learn the script before I start rehearsal. I find it useful to get it under my belt."

Meera Syal
FUNNIEST MOMENT

"Once I played a character who couldn't speak or hear. On the last night people sometimes play jokes and someone hid a fake poo inside a prop. I started to laugh and then remembered as a deaf mute, I wasn't supposed to make any noise! I had to go off-stage to get my breath back."

Ben Whishaw
BECOMING AN ACTOR

"When I was very young, I thought acting was dressing up. I dressed up, played games in costume, and put on plays and performances with my friends. I thought, 'This is what I want to do with my life.'"

SETTING THE SCENE

The set is an incredibly important part of the director and designer's vision for the play. It will be one of the first things discussed, as the look of the stage defines a play's place and atmosphere. The stage design helps tell the audience everything, from when and where the play is set to the big ideas it is exploring. Sometimes the director and designer might decide to stage a play with very little scenery, just lighting and costume. The set design will influence how the actors think about their parts and move around the stage.

VIDEO PROJECTION

Video can be an important part of the design of the set. A video designer can transform a simple physical set, using video to create scenic effects or clever illusions that would be tricky to achieve with physical scenery.

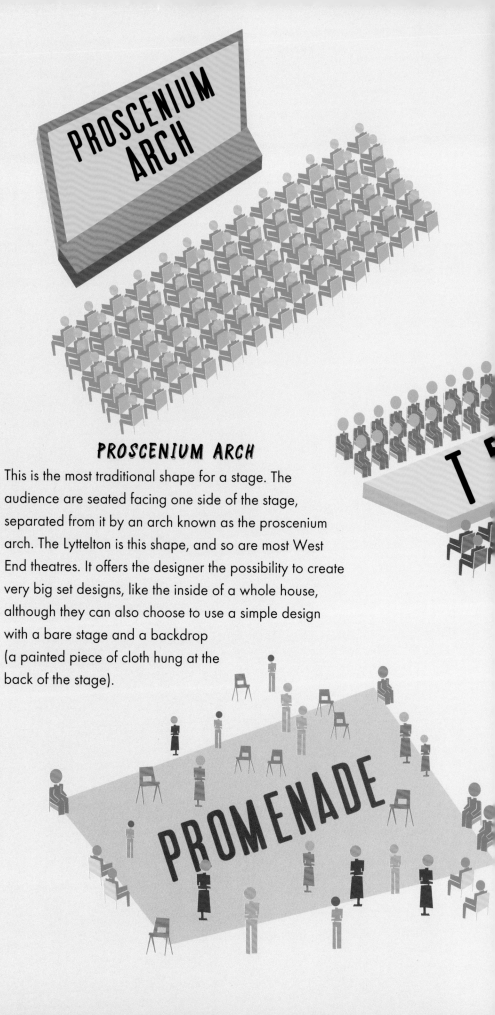

PROSCENIUM ARCH

This is the most traditional shape for a stage. The audience are seated facing one side of the stage, separated from it by an arch known as the proscenium arch. The Lyttelton is this shape, and so are most West End theatres. It offers the designer the possibility to create very big set designs, like the inside of a whole house, although they can also choose to use a simple design with a bare stage and a backdrop (a painted piece of cloth hung at the back of the stage).

DIFFERENT TYPES OF STAGE

Designers have to think about the space the play will be performed in and design the set for the shape of the theatre's stage. Often the shape of the stage will inspire the design for the set, especially if the stage has special features like the Olivier's drum revolve, which allows a section of the stage to rise, lower and rotate.

THRUST STAGE

A thrust stage extends out into the audience, so they sit on three sides of the stage. Many theatres in Shakespeare's time were built this way, including the Globe. The designer will think about the set design and how to use the thrust in a way that means all the action is visible.

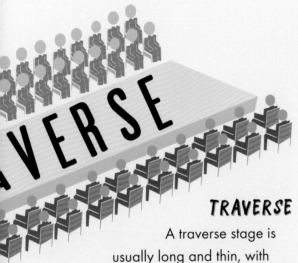

TRAVERSE

A traverse stage is usually long and thin, with the audience sitting on either side of it, facing each other. Any large scenery would need to be at the ends of the stage so the audience's view isn't obscured.

PROMENADE

In a promenade performance there is no fixed stage or auditorium. The audience sit where they like, or follow the actors around as they perform. Plays can be put on in all sorts of places apart from traditional theatres, like warehouses, churches, underground vaults and even old ships. Plays can also be staged outside, which means the designer needs to think about making the set weatherproof.

IN THE ROUND

The audience are seated on all sides of the stage when a play is staged in the round. Actors make their entrances and exits through gaps in the seats. The set will need to be cleverly thought through with more emphasis on the floor, furniture, props and costumes, so the audience can see all the action.

CREATING THE SET

Once the director and designer have agreed on the look, the designer starts sketching and making different models to see how every aspect of the set will work. They have to make sure their ideas work safely and practically. The designer also starts thinking about what the costumes and props will look like.

1 SKETCHING

A storyboard is a series of sketches which show how each scene will look. It is useful for the designer if the play requires a lot of complicated scene changes.

2 THE WHITE-CARD MODEL

The first model the designer makes is made of white card. It shows the shape and size of all the scenery inside a model of the theatre. It is built on a scale of 1:25. The designer shows the model to the producer and production manager and they share their ideas and point out problems, such as whether it will be too difficult or expensive to build.

Storyboard for
THE LIGHT PRINCESS

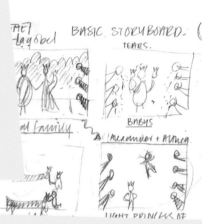

3 BALANCING THE BUDGET

Each department then works out how much it will cost to build their part of the design. The production manager will suggest ways to reduce the cost, for example by using an alternative material. Once the budget is agreed the final model is made, which will be used by all the different departments to help build the set.

4 THE FINAL MODEL

The final model is a three-dimensional map of the design. It shows everyone involved in building the set how each element should look and all the colours and textures. The designer shows it to everyone involved backstage – the stage managers, lighting and sound designers and the crew, who will be moving the set around.

The set model box for
THE LIGHT PRINCESS

Sketch and model box © Rae Smith

TREASURE ISLAND

National Theatre

TREASURE ISLAND

by Robert Louis Stevenson
adapted by Bryony Lavery

Sponsored by
Royal Bank of Canada

2014
By Robert Louis Stevenson
Adapted by Bryony Lavery
Directed by Polly Findlay
Designed by Lizzie Clachan

In **Treasure Island**, Jim discovers a treasure map and sets off to find the gold. Here, Lizzie Clachan, the designer for the National Theatre production, discusses the atmosphere she wanted the set to create:

❝ I went to Portsmouth Docks to have a look at Nelson's ship, the *Victory*. That gave me a lot of inspiration. And there was a book of cross sections of the *Victory*, which gave me the idea of doing a cross section of the ship. We decided that the stage should be dominated by a circle of huge ribs. They form the frame of the ship, but also call to mind a skeleton.

I started to look at pictures of ships in skeletal form, and I also had some Victorian pictures of whale ribs, and suddenly had the idea of using ribs as the ribs of the ship.

The Benbow Inn looks inviting, but at the same time small and vulnerable in the middle of the enormous Olivier stage, which is an epic amphitheatre. The Benbow needed to be small and cosy, but it's hard to do that on the Olivier stage. There's a balance between what the scene requires and what the stage requires. You have to use it to your advantage – so at the Benbow, we can see the pirates approaching and we know that something bad is on its way. ❞

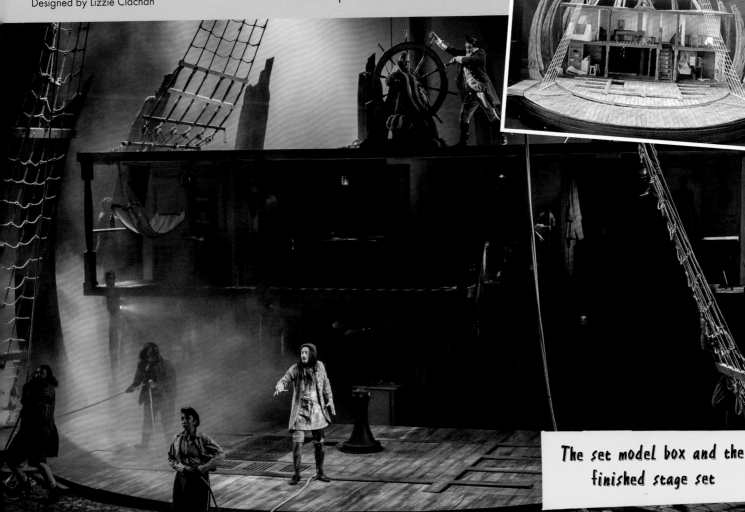

The set model box and the finished stage set

MEET THE DESIGNER

The designer is responsible for the look of everything on stage, from the set to the props.

Tim Hatley has designed many productions for the National Theatre, including **Timon of Athens**. Here, he describes what being a designer is like:

"At school my art teacher was obsessed with the theatre. He would book tickets to see whatever was on at the National Theatre. I saw in the programme there was this role of designer and I became slightly obsessed with it.

I get my inspiration through drawing and sketching and visual elements the world over. I get lots of visual materials together, because it's much easier to share your ideas when you can show something, rather than just describe it.

You start off on your own with a pencil and a large rubber. Then you share it with one other person, the director. Then it becomes public: you show your design to the theatre, and beyond. You prepare a set model as a way to share the design with everyone. Normally, you focus on the set first because that takes longest, especially on a big production. Then costume – you need to know who will be cast so you can design around their physique. Then the props.

There are great moments, but there are tough moments. I really, really enjoy it. It changes all the time. You have to become a mini expert, immerse yourself in a world. Every day is different. "

Sketch

Set model box

TIMON OF ATHENS

2012
Written by William Shakespeare
Directed by Nicholas Hytner
Designed by Tim Hatley
Dramaturg Ben Power

National Theatre
Travelex £12
Timon of Athens
by William Shakespeare

**Diane Willmott
PRODUCTION MANAGER**

The finished stage

We work closely with the designer to make their vision a reality on stage. We consider the budget and materials available and also that the design is safe for the actors and audience. As soon as the designer has something to show us, we step in and work with them towards a design that is going to achieve what they want.

BUILDING THE SET

The designer's final models are transformed into the full-size set by the construction department. Using detailed drawings, highly skilled craftsmen make the designer's vision a reality. Sets usually have to be made in pieces, so they can be moved into the theatre and then taken apart again quickly.

CONSTRUCTION

The theatre's digital drawing team turn the designer's work into construction drawings. These are very detailed and show the welders and carpenters how to build the set. Then the construction department start making the scenery from wood, metal or whatever material has been chosen. The director might ask to have some parts of the set made early to use in rehearsal.

SCENIC WORK

The scenic art department use many different materials, such as paint, plaster, rubber and plastic, to finish the set and make it look real. Scenic artists create all kinds of effects and finishes, from brick walls to broken glass and painted backdrops. Their detailed work adds to the illusion of the world of the play. To make sure the colours and textures are correct, scenic artists provide samples, which are based on a scale model of the set made by the designer.

Scenic artists also paint huge backdrops on pieces of cloth which are hung at the back of the stage. These are called cycloramas. To make sure the cloth is painted to scale the scenic artists divide the model into little squares by drawing a grid on it. They then use nails and thread to recreate the grid on the actual backdrop cloth.

THE FIT-UP

The fit-up is the final stage in the building process and happens just before the technical rehearsal. Everything is positioned and fitted together in the theatre. The lighting and sound equipment are put in place first, and then the set. It will be the first time everything has been seen together, so the designer and the rest of the creative team will be hoping there are no nasty surprises. If it doesn't look quite right there may be some last-minute adjustments.

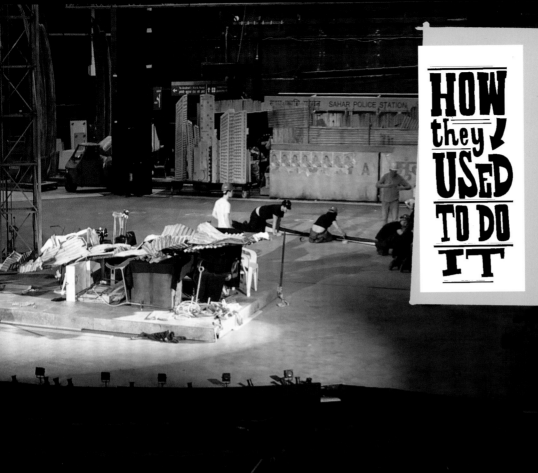

HOW they ↓ USED TO DO IT

Off-duty sailors often used to work backstage in theatres. Changing scenery involves hauling on ropes, something sailors were used to. Because of this, many words used in theatres are the same as ones you hear on boats, like 'rigging' and 'crew'. Sailors, who often came from different countries and spoke different languages, would communicate with each other using whistles. That's why it's still thought unlucky to whistle on stage – it might be the command for someone to drop a piece of scenery on an actor's head.

tricks of the trade

Scenic painters use all sorts of tricks to make things look real and solid when they aren't.

❉ Plaster and glue: applying this mixture onto a surface creates texture and makes things look worn or old. It also looks better under stage lights than a flat surface, which may be too reflective.

❉ Rubber crumbs: little bits of rubber are useful for making fake rust or mud. And because they are slightly squidgy, actors can walk on them barefoot.

❉ Brick stencils: a quick way of making a brick wall.

❉ Special brushes: a brush with a few chunks cut out of it makes the paint go on in streaks, which is good for making a surface look like wood.

❉ Foam rollers: a roller that has been slightly cut up can create a mottled effect, perfect for painting leaves and foliage.

59

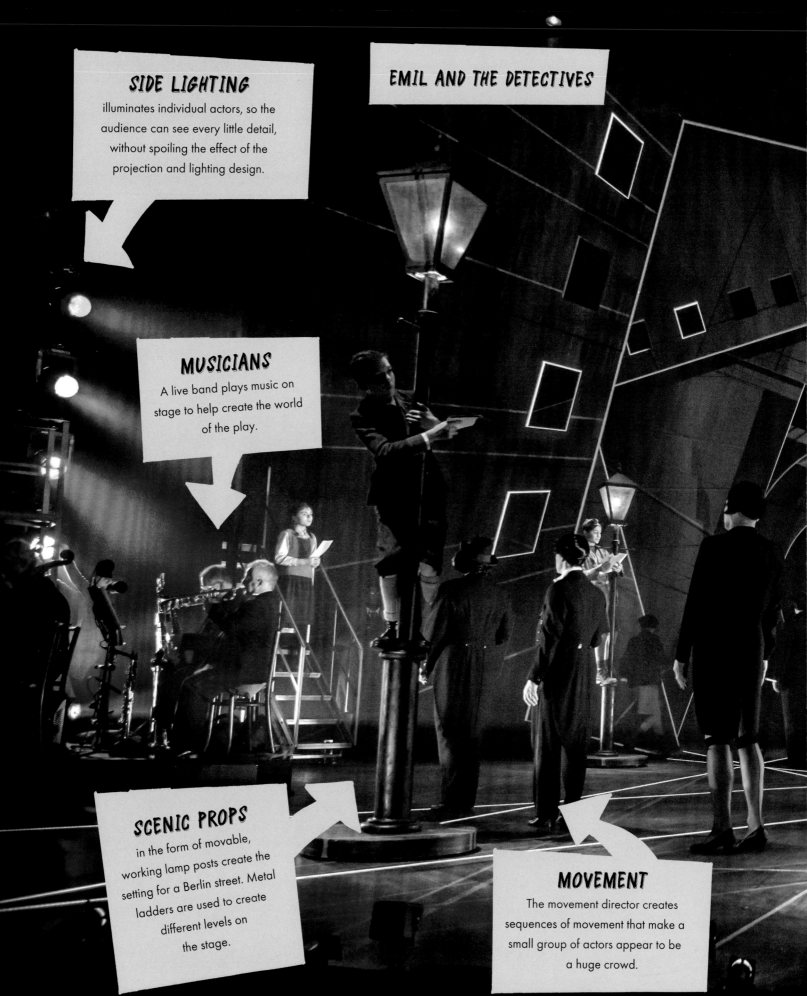

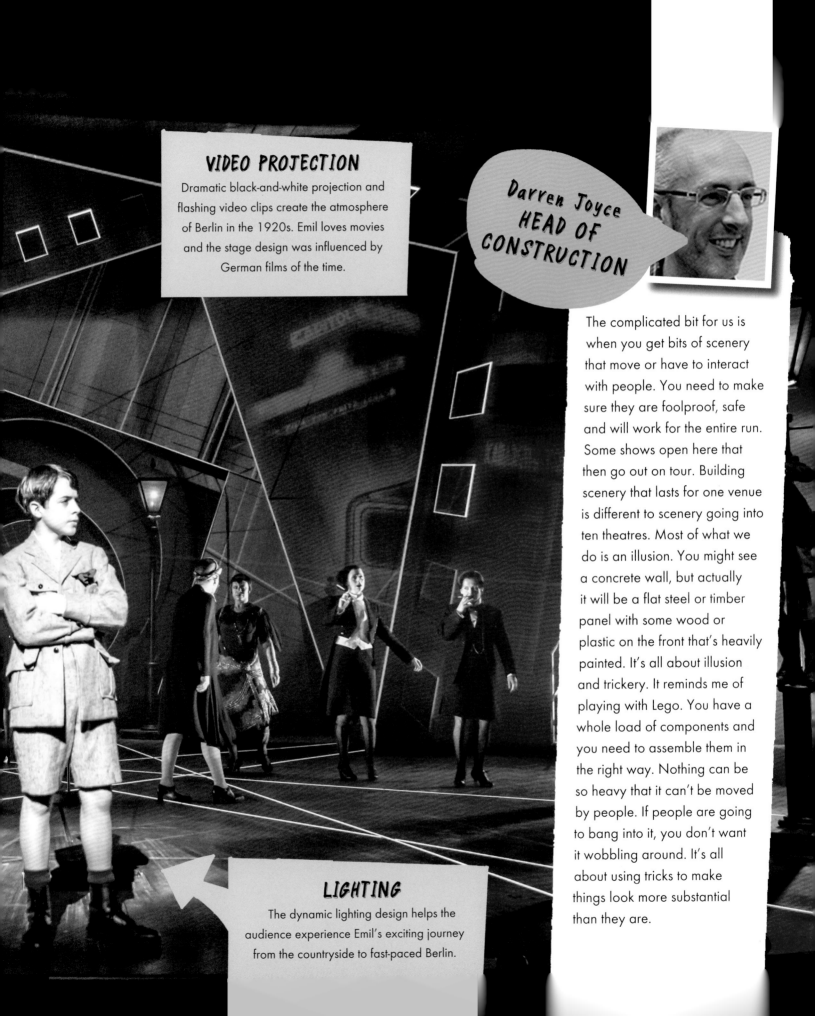

VIDEO PROJECTION

Dramatic black-and-white projection and flashing video clips create the atmosphere of Berlin in the 1920s. Emil loves movies and the stage design was influenced by German films of the time.

Darren Joyce
HEAD OF CONSTRUCTION

The complicated bit for us is when you get bits of scenery that move or have to interact with people. You need to make sure they are foolproof, safe and will work for the entire run. Some shows open here that then go out on tour. Building scenery that lasts for one venue is different to scenery going into ten theatres. Most of what we do is an illusion. You might see a concrete wall, but actually it will be a flat steel or timber panel with some wood or plastic on the front that's heavily painted. It's all about illusion and trickery. It reminds me of playing with Lego. You have a whole load of components and you need to assemble them in the right way. Nothing can be so heavy that it can't be moved by people. If people are going to bang into it, you don't want it wobbling around. It's all about using tricks to make things look more substantial than they are.

LIGHTING

The dynamic lighting design helps the audience experience Emil's exciting journey from the countryside to fast-paced Berlin.

THE DRUM REVOLVE

At the heart of the Olivier's stage is a piece of machinery that's only found at the National Theatre. It's called a drum revolve and it allows the designer to create all sorts of amazing effects.

The drum revolve allows a circular section in the middle of the stage to spin around. That circle also splits into two semi-circles, and one side can rise up out of the stage or sink down into it. The whole rotating cylinder reaches five storeys below the stage.

Sets can be changed quickly just by swivelling whatever was at the back of the stage to the front. Scenery can also be built on one of the semi-circular sections, so a new world is revealed when it rises up out of the stage. The revolve can also be used to create clever illusions. If actors walk on it while it turns in the opposite direction, they stay in the same place, or if they walk in the same direction it will look as if they are travelling at double speed.

Lizzie Clachan
DESIGNER

The drum revolve is quite complicated to use. There are weight limits to consider, and because two or three productions perform alternately on the stage (which is called repertory), set items also have to be stored. You want to try to use all that machinery in a way that's visually interesting. Using it to move the set from one side to the other doesn't feel magical or interesting. But the revolve can also be like a ballet, like dancing machinery.

②

The Olivier's crew test the drum revolve while resetting the stage

TREASURE ISLAND

National Theatre

TREASURE
ISLAND

by Robert Louis Stevenson
adapted by Bryony Lavery

Sponsored by
RBC   Royal Bank of Canada

2014
By Robert Louis Stevenson
Adapted by Bryony Lavery
Directed by Polly Findlay
Designed by Lizzie Clachan

In **Treasure Island**, the drum revolve was used to create the Benbow Inn, the home of Jim Hawkins, and then a ship. For the ship, the drum revolve rose out of the stage to reveal a cross section of the cabins below deck.

COSTUME

THE IMPORTANCE OF COSTUME

**Lizzie Clachan
DESIGNER**

Costumes help the designer create the world of the play, showing the audience when and where it is set. They are carefully chosen, as everything an actor wears tells the audience about their character, revealing all sorts of things about their age, job, relationship with other characters and position in society.

I knew I had to design the costumes imaginatively and cheaply for **Treasure Island**. The National Theatre has a massive store of costumes and we got lots of them and put things together, making alterations, adding this sleeve on to that jacket. It was a crazy mash-up – the most fun costume thing I'd ever done. Even though **Treasure Island** is set in the 18th century, we didn't want to be slaves to that. The costumes go right up to the 1940s, and Jim, the main character, wears a pair of trousers that were based on the trackie bottoms that the actor wore to rehearsals. We had some ideas for one of the pirates, Killigrew the Kind. But when I went to see a run-through, his whole character had developed. I suddenly had a vision for how the character should look. I saw him as a kind of butcher, and I thought he needed a tight butcher's coat. So we had to scrap what we had made for the actor and start again.

PERIOD OR MODERN?

Costumes are part of the director's and designer's vision for the play and are a way to explore and highlight certain issues in a play.

If a play is set in the past, the designer has to decide whether they want the costumes to be from that particular historical period. Traditionally, plays set in the past were almost always performed in period costume. Today, designers can use modern costumes for plays set in the past or period costumes for a play set in the present day, or a mixture of costumes from all different periods. It all depends on the message they want the clothes to convey.

If a designer decides to use authentic period costumes, this can turn the play into a fascinating and believable portrait of a particular time. But using modern dress for a play set in the past can help the audience make connections between that period and their own life and times. For instance, having the soldiers in Shakespeare's **Henry V**, which is set in medieval times, wear modern army uniform might make the audience feel that war hasn't changed over the centuries.

Sometimes the designer might decide to make the costumes not from any recognizable historical period, but to keep them simple and plain. This can help make the play seem universal and timeless and encourage the audience to use their imaginations.

STATS & FACTS

The National Theatre has 75,000 costumes from every style and period imaginable, from medieval cloaks and 1920s dresses to modern jeans.

SEWING

Costume is incredibly important in building a character. You have a chat with the costume designer, and they may have picked out a rail of clothes to try. Sometimes they take you shopping. I love wearing period costumes, because it feels like that little bit further to go for a story. It's just the storyteller in me, I suppose.

CREATING CHARACTER

Costumes help actors get into their character. They can also alter an actor's physical appearance. Padding can make an actor fatter, or a corset can achieve a tiny waist. If the designer has chosen period costumes, actors sometimes wear long skirts and corsets from the first day of rehearsals to get a feeling for what it was like to wear them.

GETTING THE LOOK

Because costumes can change the way an actor performs, the designer starts by talking to the actors. Some will have very strong feelings about what their character's costume should be, so the designer may then find images – from a magazine or a work of art – to help give an idea of the right colours and mood. Clothes will be gathered up from the theatre's costume store or from charity shops, so actors can try them on and see what works. Some designers love using old clothes that have a bit of history, while others want everything to be brand-new.

tricks of the trade

There are various ways to make costumes look old and worn, even if they are brand-new. This process is called 'breaking down' and is done by the team in the Dye Shop, who also create patterns, dye fabric and add texture to costumes. To break down material, the Dye Shop team rub in Vaseline or wax, or put soap on the collar and cuffs to make them look greasy. Or they rub the fabric with sandpaper to roughen it up. They might even carefully burn the hems or stretch the pockets by filling them with damp newspaper.

CREATIVE COSTUME

Costumes are made in all sorts of different ways by the costume department. Sometimes they are made especially for a play. Sometimes the costume department will cleverly adapt costumes that have been made for another play or buy ready-made clothes from shops.

SECRET STITCHING

The costume department have to make the costumes look as authentic as possible, but also make sure they are practical and comfortable for the actors. Even costumes that look like normal clothes may hold secrets. Sometimes the pockets are made extra deep to carry props. The patterns and colours may be a tiny bit brighter and bolder, so they look good from a distance under the stage lights. Costumes are usually made to be stronger than normal clothes too, with extra strong seams and tougher materials, so that actors can run and jump without tearing them. Each actor will have a costume fitting for every costume to check that the fit is perfect.

TRY THIS AT HOME

Think carefully about what each costume will say about each character in the play. Make a mood board with different ideas and think about the colour, texture and shape of each item. Charity shops are great places to look. Try stitching on ribbons, feathers or sequins to clothes or ripping and dirtying them to get new looks.

KEEPING CLEAN

Once the play is being performed in the theatre, the running wardrobe team are responsible for making sure the costumes look good for every single performance. They will repair any damaged ones and also make sure they are clean each night. Acting under bright lights can be hot and sweaty, so if an actor is wearing an outfit that can't be washed easily, such as a heavy overcoat, they will wear a T-shirt underneath that can be washed after every performance. Two versions of the same outfit can be made if an actor has to look clean in one scene and dirty in the next, to avoid washing the grime out every night.

Steve Walker
WARDROBE SUPERVISOR

A quick change can be a crazy adrenaline rush. Often the changes are in complete darkness. There might be two people doing the change. One gets the trousers and shoes off, one's waiting with the other trousers. You have everything laid out. Often you will have someone from hair and make-up there and you're falling over each other. Sometimes we go on stage in costume to do a change, so we blend in with the actors. Normally we are tucked behind a piece of set, or rush on during a scene change when it's dark. If the audience could see what's going on backstage, it would be more of a show than the show!

AGAINST THE CLOCK

Dressers from the running wardrobe team also help actors make quick costume changes off-stage. If the change has to be really quick, the costume might be made with Velcro, poppers or magnets to come apart quickly. Actors also often wear layers of clothes to make quick changes. They just have to take off the top layer and underneath is a whole new outfit ready for the next scene.

Getting ready for a quick change

69

Anne-Marie Duff
ACTOR

The costume that stands out most for me has to be the bespoke suit of armour that I wore for **Saint Joan**. I had never worn anything like that before and it had a profound effect on the scenes that I played wearing it. Wearing it made me feel very powerful and very heavy.

FROM SKETCH TO STAGE

The costume department will take the designer's sketches and transform them into incredible costumes that perfectly fit each actor. Sometimes the sketches will be just a rough outline of the designer's vision. At other times they will have detailed ideas for colours and textures.

Sketch © Rae Smith

Althea's regal costume made from luxurious fabrics in THE LIGHT PRINCESS

Victor's costume in FRANKENSTEIN when he creates the Creature

The most spectacular costume I ever wore was definitely for Atahuallpa, the king of the Incas, in **The Royal Hunt of the Sun**. The costume was so massive I couldn't even see it all when I was in it. There was a huge headdress with feathers, beautifully made. It had a cloak that made me look enormous.

The chorus, dressed as Victorian dandies, in the farce THE MAGISTRATE

THEATRE WORDS

The **CHORUS** is a group of actors who describe and comment on the main action of the play. It dates back to very early Ancient Greek theatre.

EMIL AND THE DETECTIVES

2013
By Erich Kästner
Adapted by Carl Miller
Directed by Bijan Sheibani
Designed by Bunny Christie

In **Emil and the Detectives**, Emil leaves his home in the countryside and, after getting his money stolen on the train, pursues the thief on the streets of bustling 1920s Berlin. He's helped by a group of city children. For their costumes, Bunny Christie, the designer, did lots of research. The costumes had to reflect all the different characters' very distinct personalities. Emil was dressed in traditional German dress, and his clothes looked old-fashioned next to the sharper and trendier Berlin children.

National Theatre

EMIL
AND THE
DETECTIVES

by Erich Kästner
adapted by Carl Miller

EMIL

GERDA

TOOTS

TUESDAY

Ernst Toby Daniel

EMIL

GERDA

TOOTS

Stuart McQuarrie

MR SNOW

Keyaan —— Johnny —— Nathaniel

TUESDAY

WIGS,

HAIR & KE-UP

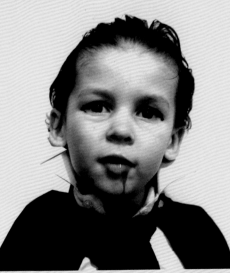

WIGS AND HAIR

Wigs can make an actor look and feel the part, by giving them hair in a different style, colour or length. They tell the audience a lot about the characters and the play's setting. Wigs can also help actors quickly change role or show them ageing during the play's action.

The wig team will meet with the designer and director to discuss how the actors' hair will look throughout the play. They might decide that an elaborate hairstyle can be created just using an actor's real hair and some hairpieces. If the wig team decide a wig is needed, they make sure that it matches the actor's colouring and fits perfectly, so it doesn't fall off. Most of the time the audience will never realize an actor is wearing a wig.

Curling hair on a wig

MAKING THE CUT

Human hair, which looks most realistic, is used for many theatrical wigs. Wigs are expensive, around £1,000 each, but sometimes old wigs can be restyled and then used for another play. Wig makers start by measuring the actor's head and creating an exact copy by wrapping it in clingfilm and then sticky tape. Ready-made models, called head blocks, can then be padded until they are exactly the right size and shape. A thin net, called a lace, is stitched to form a foundation, and tiny amounts of hair are knotted into it, sometimes a single hair at a time. It's fiddly, delicate work, and it takes one person at least five days to create a wig. It can take even longer for really difficult wigs like the ones worn by lawyers and judges.

A wig on stage

When I played Cordelia in **King Lear** I asked if I could have brown hair. I didn't recognize myself in the wig, and I really loved that. If I could, I would wear a wig for every part. Transforming is a huge part of what it's about for me.

BEARDS AND MOUSTACHES

The wig team also have to make fake moustaches, beards and sideburns. These have to match the colour of the actor's wig. They are made from scratch and stored by type in a special folder. And it's not just facial hair. The wig team might even have to make armpit or chest hair for an actor.

MAKE-UP

Make-up can change an actor's face, making them look older, younger or completely different. It is mostly used to emphasize features such as eyes and lips, making it easier for the audience to read the actors' expressions from a distance. Many theatres have make-up artists who decide with the designer on what make-up the actors should wear.

If an actor only needs simple make-up – just a bit of eyeliner and lipstick – they will usually apply it themselves, sometimes with a bit of guidance from a professional. But the WH&M (Wigs, Hair and Make-up) department will step in if special effects make-up is needed to create wounds or blood, or if prosthetics, such as big ears or crooked noses, are being used. One day a make-up artist might be making someone look pretty, and the next turning someone into a monster.

PROSTHETICS

Make-up artists use amazing products like silicone and latex to mould actors new features, to make them look ill or dirty and to create scars, bruises, blood and dirt. You can even buy whole prosthetic latex foreheads, noses and chins. Other special effects can be done with normal make-up. Make-up artists can change the shape of someone's face by putting new shadows in the creases, changing the contours.

Applying special effects make-up can take hours. Some actors find it relaxing. They can focus on getting into the part as their character takes shape in the mirror before them.

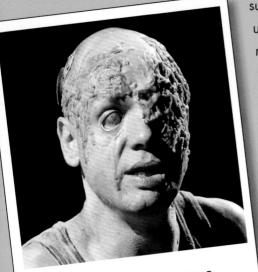

Prosthetics on stage

HOW they USED TO DO IT

Have you heard the expression "being in the limelight"? In Victorian times, theatres were lit by heating blocks of quicklime to very high temperatures. They gave off an intense light, known as limelight, and actors had to wear heavy, bold make-up so you could see their faces properly. These days, stage make-up is much more subtle because stage lighting is less harsh, and audiences are used to watching TV and expect a more natural look.

FRANKENSTEIN

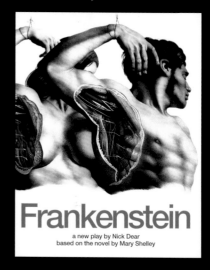

Frankenstein

a new play by Nick Dear
based on the novel by Mary Shelley

2011
A new play by Nick Dear
Based on the novel by Mary Shelley
Directed by Danny Boyle
Set designed by Mark Tildesley
Costumes designed by Suttirat Anne Larlarb

Frankenstein tells the story of a scientist, Frankenstein, who makes a creature from bits of dead bodies and then brings it to life using electricity. Frankenstein is horrified by his creation and adandons it. The Creature decides to track down Frankenstein and get his terrible revenge.

For the production directed by Danny Boyle at the National Theatre, Benedict Cumberbatch and Jonny Lee Miller took it in turns to play the Creature and Frankenstein at each performance. Their wigs and make-up had to look identical. The Creature had to look as if it had

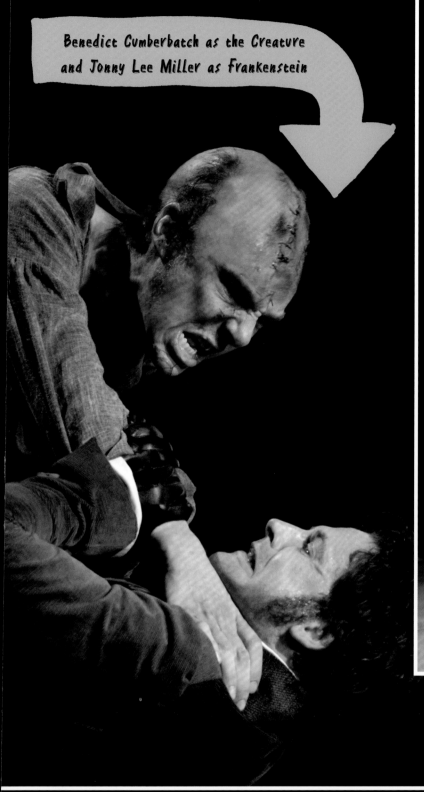

Benedict Cumberbatch as the Creature and Jonny Lee Miller as Frankenstein

Clever prosthetics helped the two actors to swap roles for every performance

Giuseppe Cannas
HEAD OF WH&M

been stitched together from dead bodies. Before each performance, whichever actor was playing the Creature spent hours in the make-up chair having scars, wounds and huge stitches applied. The Creature was also almost bald, with only a few ugly tufts of hair on his head, and his skin was the purpley colour of a corpse. And the make-up didn't just go on the actor's face, but his whole body, because in the first scene of the play the Creature is naked.

Frankenstein was a massive undertaking, a two-hour make-up call every night, compared to the usual half hour. It wasn't just prosthetics, we also had to cover up Jonny's tattoos.

79

If you want to create your own stage make-up, you first need to do some research, especially if you are thinking about recreating a particular style or period. Try making a mood board of different pictures and ideas. Then use this kit to create all sorts of different effects.

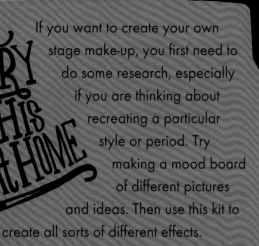

TRY THIS AT HOME

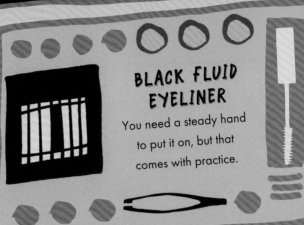

BLACK FLUID EYELINER

You need a steady hand to put it on, but that comes with practice.

STAGE MAKE-UP

This is thicker than normal make-up: thick enough to cover birthmarks and tattoos. You can buy it in theatre supply shops and on the internet, but if you can't find any, have a go with ordinary face paints.

BRUSHES IN DIFFERENT SIZES

The bigger the area you are working on, the bigger the brush you need. Little brushes are great for tiny areas like the corners of lips and eyes.

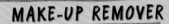

MAKE-UP REMOVER

Unless you want to stay that way!

MAKE-UP SPONGES

You can get different textured ones for different effects.

FACE POWDER

If you are using colourful make-up, try to find colourless powder so it doesn't clash. Face powder keeps the make-up in place so it won't run if you sweat.

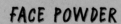

DARK EYESHADOW

Changing the shadows around the eyes will alter the whole face.

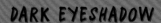

1 For a witch, you need three colours – one medium, one light and one dark. We used green, yellow and dark blue. Using a big brush, cover the face in your base colour (green in this case). You want it to look thick and even all over, including the lips.

2 With a slightly smaller brush, apply the lighter colour (yellow) to areas you want to highlight – the cheekbones, the area just under the eyebrows, between the eyebrows, a line down the middle of the nose and the middle of the chin. Use a sponge to blend it in.

HOW TO DO A WITCH'S FACE

3 Next come the shadows. Put a little of the darker colour (blue) under the cheekbones, down the sides of the nose, in the creases of the eyelids and the crease just above the chin. Use a sponge to blend again.

4 Put some powder on to keep everything in place. Apply it with a powder puff, then smooth it out with a big clean brush.

5 Use a stipple sponge – one with a rough texture – to put a bit more yellow and blue over the highlights and shadows. Stipple sponges pick up more colour so they intensify the effect.

6 Using a tiny brush, draw a yellow line in the inner corners of the eyes and around the outside of the lips, especially the cupid's bow at the top.

7 Put some black eyeliner around the eyes, as close as possible to the eyelashes. Be bold – a thick line looks more dramatic – but try to get it on in a smooth sweep. Use more eyeliner to draw over the eyebrows and around the inside edge of the lips. Sweep on some dark eyeshadow in the eyelid creases.

Ta-da!
A witch. We used a wig and hat to complete the look.

PICKING THE RIGHT PROPS

A prop is an object handled by an actor on stage. Props help create the play's atmosphere and setting and can be very important to the way the play's story unfolds. An object like a letter or a gun can be critical at a particular point in a plot. The designer will decide what the props will look like and how they will help tell the story. The props department will then find or make the different props. They can be big or small, cheap or expensive, ordinary or extraordinary.

Eleanor Smith & Kirsten Shiell PROPS SUPERVISORS

We organize all the props, furniture and set dressing. We work with the creative team and actors during rehearsals to work out what the play needs. The best thing is the variety. A prop can be from any period in time or from any country in the world. We get to be creative, but also need to be practical.

REAL RESEARCH

Once the set design has been agreed, the designer will start to think about the smaller details that help make the set look real and tell the story of the play. The props department will help the designer with the look of the different types of prop. It can take hours of research. It would break the illusion if a prop was from the wrong historical period or gave the wrong impression about the mood and tone of a particular scene.

The props department then have to consider carefully how they will make the props. A glass might need to smash in a dramatic way or a play might need a working chandelier. The props might have to look very expensive, like a golden throne or a big mahogany dining table, but they can't always be in real life. The props department also have to consider the needs of the actors and the crew. If a prop is too heavy it could make it difficult for an actor to carry it around the stage or make it harder for the crew to change the scene.

A prop's development from rehearsals to opening night

DIFFERENT TYPES OF PROPS

Soft props are made of material – things like bedclothes, curtains and drapes.

Costume props are props that are worn, such as armour, hats and jewellery.

Set dressing props are props that are important to the look of the set but aren't handled by the actors. These can also be practical parts of the set that need to work, like electrical lights or running water.

Hand props are small props that are carried by the actors and necessary for the action, like a letter or a glass.

Scenic props are props that are so large they are considered part of the scenery, like trees. The props and set departments may work together on these.

Personal props help an actor develop their character, like a pipe or walking stick.

Rehearsal props
Props can be very important to the dramatic action of the play, so actors will often want something similar to what they will be using on stage to practise with during rehearsals. They might also want to practise with their personal props so they can make sure they are as much a part of their character as possible.

INSIDE THE PROPS DEPARTMENT

Once the list of props has been agreed for a production, the props department decide which ones should be made, bought or adapted from existing props. Usually the decision about where a prop should come from depends on how much time there is and what is affordable.

FINDING AND CRAFTING

The props department have many different skills – from carpentry to sewing to painting. The magic of props is all about making things look like what they are not. In the props workshop, foam, latex and polystyrene are disguised to look like wood or stone through tricks such as the clever use of paint.

Sometimes it's easier to buy a prop than make one from scratch, especially if it's something ordinary like a book, table or chair. Junkyards, antique markets, specialist shops and the internet are all good places to look. For plays set in the present day, it's often easier and cheaper to buy things than make them.

Or the props department will buy a piece of furniture that is similar to what the designer wants and adapt it – for instance, by painting it a different colour or covering it in different fabric.

THE PROPS LIST

For the National Theatre's production of **Treasure Island**, the props department had to make all kinds of props, from tiny coins to much bigger pieces of furniture, and make sure they were right for the action of the play. For example, an old sea-chest had to look heavy and ancient, but Jim's grandmother had to be able to swing it on to her shoulder easily. This list shows some of the things that were needed.

HOW they USED TO DO IT

A medieval morality play called **The Castle of Perseverance**, written in about 1425, is the first to mention props (or 'propyrtes', in medieval spelling). A prologue, or opening speech, promises that props will be used in the play.

TREASURE ISLAND PROPS LIST

1 miniature ship

15 interesting tankards

1 old and shabby chair

1 shell-encrusted chair

1 treasure chest containing coins and old papers

1 music box that plays a haunting tune

1 treasure map

Framed paintings of royalty

1 telescope

1 globe

1 compass

1 parrot cage

1 large, hanging ham

Gunpowder barrels

2 Jolly Roger flags

1 rusty pistol

PERFECT PROPS

A great prop will look convincing from where the audience are sitting, even if it is obviously fake close up. And the actors and the crew need to be able to handle it. Here are a few brilliant props made by the National Theatre's props department.

This dead deer was made for **King Lear** out of layers of foam and fake fur. It was so realistic that some people wrote in to complain, thinking it was an actual deer.

Making the deer

Puppets can also be important props. They are made from all sorts of materials, from wood to metal or plastic. They must look and move realistically on stage.

Dog in Handspring Puppet Company's OR YOU COULD KISS ME, which could wag its tail

This cannon was used in **The Silver Tassie**, a play set during the First World War. It looks like it is made of heavy, solid metal, but that would have made it hard for the actors to drag it on stage – and much too expensive. Instead, it is made of a mixture of materials including card and foam, painted to look muddy.

Arthur Darvill
ACTOR

Props are really important to developing performances. Sometimes it can be a hindrance to have too much stuff. Other times it can be great because they can be really good tools for telling the story. I'm quite clumsy, and it takes me a while to get used to using props – until I make sure I can't break them. Once you get used to them, they become a great friend. There's a ladle in **Treasure Island**, which was for ages the bane of my life. I didn't know what to do with it! Then it became a useful tool, a pointing tool: I used it to show my intentions.

The finished cannon on stage

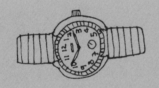

tricks of the trade

If actors eat food on stage, it has to be real food. But if nobody eats it, it makes more sense to make fake food – otherwise it would soon get smelly and be very wasteful. Sometimes it is made from a mould of the real thing. If characters drink alcohol on stage, soft drinks are used instead, such as ginger ale for champagne.

PROPS IN PERFORMANCE

It can be very busy behind the scenes during a performance. Actors are coming on and off the stage, often changing their costumes, and the crew are busy with the set and scenery. The stage managers make sure all the right props are in the right places, which is not always an easy job.

THE PROPS TABLE

It would be a disaster if an actor walked on stage without the sword they needed for a scene where they were about to have a fight. To stop any actor going on stage without the right props, there is a table off-stage in the wings with a space marked out in tape for every prop that gets carried on stage by an actor. One of the stage managers (usually the assistant stage manager, or ASM) will be responsible for making sure everything is where the actors need it to be before the play starts. The ASM will also check that the props are ready for the play, as a wine glass might need to be filled with wine or a candle lit on a birthday cake.

A props table

Fake food ready to be used on stage

The props store at the National Theatre

PROPS ON STAGE

Sometimes a prop might need to be smashed or broken on stage as part of the action of the play. Often this means the props department will have to have enough versions of that prop to last the entire run of performances. The props department will adapt each prop so the moment on stage looks as dramatic as possible. If a vase is supposed to break on stage but is quite sturdy, prop makers may put little cracks in it with a hammer beforehand to make sure it really will shatter. Real glass doesn't usually get used on stage because it's too dangerous. Plastic can be used instead, or resin if it needs to smash.

Sometimes the props department will make a prop that can be broken every night and then put back together again. In **Treasure Island**, Jim's grandmother sits in a chair that later gets smashed to pieces by the marauding pirates. It was cleverly made to come apart when the actor who picks it up releases a clip, with other parts held together with magnets. By the time the pirates are finished with it, it looks like splintered bits of wood. But when the next performance begins, it is ready to be a chair again.

AFTER THE FINAL CURTAIN

If a prop is huge and never likely to be used again, it may be taken apart and recycled. But the National Theatre also has a vast warehouse of props from plays that have finished. Many props will end up there, and may be used again and again, or altered and adapted for plays in the future.

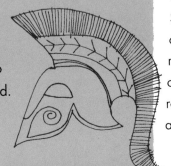

Cynthia Duberr
STAGE MANAGER

It's normally things that break, especially when it's a one-off, that make you nervous. Or something small getting lost. As soon as the actor comes off stage you're there going: 'Hi, I'll take that off your hands!' They always laugh – actors are aware of what it's like. We have lots of knives and daggers in **The James Plays**, plays about Scottish kings, and the actors run off stage and go to their dressing rooms, and then you have to collect them all. We create a routine to keep all the props safe and in the right place.

MAKING THE IMPOSSIBLE POSSIBLE

One of the most exciting things about watching a play is that something that seems impossible can suddenly happen, often at an important moment in the story. Behind the scenes, specialist teams carefully plan, create and rehearse all kinds of special effects, including fires, explosions, storms and even actors flying or bleeding to death.

EXPLOSIONS

Big fireballs on stage, like this one in **The Silver Tassie**, are usually made with propane, a flammable gas, which comes out through a tube and is ignited. Actors need to stand well out of the way. An explosion without flames can be created by using compressed air to fire bits of harmless foam or cork that look like debris on to the stage. Both those methods look impressive but don't create much sound, so the explosions have to be set off at the same time as something called a concussion pot. This is a bit like a massive firecracker and gives the explosion a bang sound. A smoke machine can then be used to create smoke on stage.

There are also tricks that let actors set themselves on fire. But if an actor has to repeat the trick for every single performance, it is likely that someone will get hurt. Often, special effects make-up will be applied quickly to the actor, so it looks as if they have been burned instead.

WHEN THINGS GO WRONG

During a performance of **The Silver Tassie**, an explosion set fire to a piece of scenery as it was being lifted off stage. The play had to be stopped while the fire was put out.

FLYING

At the National Theatre, the Olivier and Lyttelton theatres both have systems that allow actors to fly on invisible wires. The Olivier's system is particularly sophisticated and can carry actors backwards and forwards, left and right. Each of its hoists can carry 200kg, the weight of about three adults, and can even lift big bits of scenery. Flying is essential for plays like **The Light Princess** (which was in the Lyttelton), a fairy-tale where a weightless princess floats through the air.

BRAVING THE ELEMENTS

To make it look like it is windy, the special effects team use a wind machine. The machine has an incredibly powerful fan, which blows air on to the stage. Fog machines can also be used to create a hazy effect. They freeze carbon dioxide or nitrogen gas to create the fog.

Rain on stage comes through sprinklers. But the stage mustn't get slippery and waterlogged or flood the theatre. The stage has to be covered in something waterproof like lino, which is full of little holes for the water to go through. Underneath the stage, the water is collected in troughs.

Fake snow can be made in several different ways. Pieces of white plastic can be dropped down on to the stage, a bit like confetti. This is good because it means the stage doesn't get slippery, though it can be messy to clear up. Snow machines use a special fluid to create white foam bubbles that melt as they touch the stage.

DYING

Many tragedies end with people dying on stage. The highest number of deaths in a single Shakespeare play is fourteen in **Titus Andronicus**. It's an important skill to be able to die convincingly on stage. And after an actor has died, they must stay very, very still or they will ruin the illusion for the audience. There are several different ways the special effects team help to make dying look convincing.

BLEEDING ON STAGE

If an actor needs to bleed from a wound, they keep a small squeezy bulb of fake blood in a pocket, with a tube leading to wherever they need to bleed from, for instance their chest if their character gets stabbed in the heart. Squeezing the bulb makes the blood travel along the tube and out of the wound. Fake blood is made from special chemicals that won't hurt skin and can be easily washed off.

KNIVES

A retractable knife is great for pretending to stab someone. When the knife touches the skin, the blade is pushed back into the handle so it seems to disappear.

With a blood knife an actor can make it look as if the blade has sliced the skin. The handle of the knife is filled with fake blood. As the knife is held against the skin, the handle is squeezed and blood oozes out from an invisible slit in the blade.

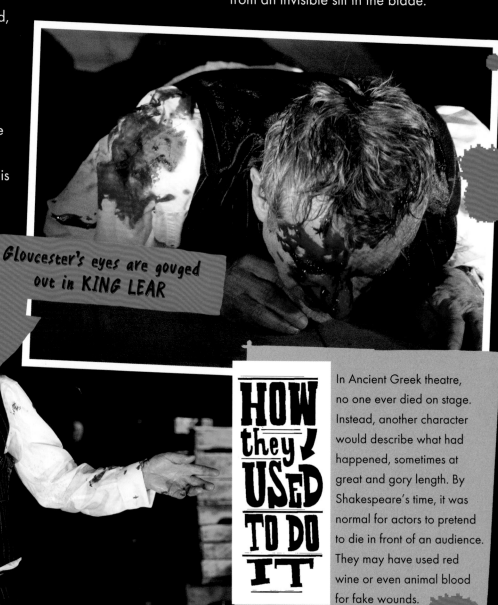

Gloucester's eyes are gouged out in KING LEAR

HOW they USED TO DO IT

In Ancient Greek theatre, no one ever died on stage. Instead, another character would describe what had happened, sometimes at great and gory length. By Shakespeare's time, it was normal for actors to pretend to die in front of an audience. They may have used red wine or even animal blood for fake wounds.

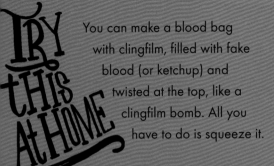
You can make a blood bag with clingfilm, filled with fake blood (or ketchup) and twisted at the top, like a clingfilm bomb. All you have to do is squeeze it.

Kate Waters
FIGHT DIRECTOR

You can use fake blood in different ways. The secret is not showing the audience how it is done. Sometimes we put a blood pack – a pouch of fake blood – on the actor, so they can squeeze it when they get stabbed. Or we hide blood bags in the set, so the actor can pick it up and squeeze it on themselves at the right moment. But fake blood is slippery and can be a hazard.

Anna Maxwell Martin
ACTOR

Dying on stage is awful! In **King Lear** we came up with lots of ideas for ways to die. One idea was sitting in a chair, but that's agony as you're sitting there for a long time! I managed to persuade Sam Mendes, the director, that I could go and die under a table instead.

ARMOURY

Lots of plays need actors to carry swords, knives and guns, and make the audience believe that somebody is shot or stabbed. The armoury and special effects team have to make sure that the weapons look real and sound convincing, but can't hurt anyone. When the National Theatre uses guns on stage, they have been adapted so they can't fire real bullets. Some fire blanks, while others can't fire anything at all. Even though they aren't real, weapons are used very carefully on stage, with lots of rehearsal.

STATS & FACTS

There are 400 guns and about 300 swords from all different periods of history in the National Theatre's armoury. The weapons are all either fake or decommissioned.

tricks of the trade

Lighting is one of the most important tools for creating atmosphere on stage.

Releasing smoke means the audience can see the beams of light in the air and this can create the effect of sunlight or dust.

If part of the set is made from gauze, it will look solid if you shine a light on it from the front. But if you light it from the back, the gauze will be see-through. That can be useful if you want to reveal what is going on behind a wall.

Pepper's Ghost is an old lighting trick used to make spooky apparitions on stage. An actor stands hidden in the wings, with a piece of glass on stage angled towards them (the audience shouldn't be able to see the glass). When light is shone on the actor, they are reflected in the glass and seem to appear out of nowhere.

Pepper's Ghost in action

SHINE BRIGHT

All theatres need lights to illuminate the stage. Only outdoor theatres, such as the Globe, use natural daylight. But lighting does much more than just show the audience what's going on. It helps tell the story by setting the scene and creating a mood. It can create atmospheric effects like lightning or a helicopter searchlight. Lighting can also make an entirely new and strange world for the audience to experience.

THE VISION

The lighting designer decides exactly how lighting should be used in the production. After they have read the script, they will talk to the director and designer about how lighting can strengthen their vision. In **Frankenstein**, for example, Bruno Poet's lighting was very important. Thousands of different shaped lightbulbs were hung from a mirrored ceiling. Frankenstein brings his Creature to life using electricity, and the shining lightbulbs made this a dazzling moment. The bulbs also suggested the Industrial Revolution, the period when the play is set. The lighting designer will go to rehearsals to see exactly how the actors move around the stage and how the lighting signals, or cues, will work.

VIDEO PROJECTION

Productions also sometimes use video footage projected onto the scenery to create different effects that build the play's mood and atmosphere. The video designer will work with the designers and develop the projections. In **Here Lies Love**, a musical about the former First Lady of the Philippines, Imelda Marcos, video design was used to create the world of the play. Real news footage from Imelda Marcos' life was projected onto all four sides of the theatre, creating a constantly changing set.

Try this At Home

* See what different effects you can make using torches with clear coloured sweet wrappers taped over the light end.
* A torch held under your chin in the dark looks creepy.
* Twinkly fairy lights with all the other lights in the room switched off can create a disco effect.
* Try hanging up a bedsheet and lighting it from behind, then see what effects you can make with shadows.

Mark Henderson's lighting design and Bob Crowley's set for THE HARD PROBLEM

Finn Ross
VIDEO DESIGNER

Lighting helps us to see the environment and the people on stage, and it adds warmth and atmosphere. Video gives us a strong graphic picture that lighting can't always achieve. Both capture the audience's imagination.

LET THERE BE LIGHTS

All technical effects, including the drum revolve at the National Theatre, can be programmed in advance by computer, so all the operator has to do is press a button for the next change to happen. Every light on stage, and there could be hundreds of them, has a number, which corresponds to a numbered channel on a lighting desk, often at the back of the theatre. The lighting operator can turn all the lights on and off using those switches.

Lights that are part of the set are also controlled by the lighting desk. If an actor walks into a room and turns on a light switch, that switch is probably not real; instead, the operator will turn on the light at the same time. Responding to what the actors are doing in this way is called using a visual cue.

If actors walk on stage carrying lanterns or torches, those will also be operated from the lighting desk, but the lights inside them are controlled wirelessly, or the trailing wires would ruin the effect.

TIMINGS ON THE NIGHT

The lighting department do a rig check every night before a show to make sure every single light is working, including the ones backstage that the audience can't see.

During the performance the deputy stage manager, known as the DSM, is responsible for making sure the visual cues all happen at the right time. They sit either in the wings or at the back of the theatre with a copy of the script that has every single cue marked in it. Each cue has a number. When the moment comes, the DSM will say into a radio relay system, "Cue 53 – go". That sends the message to the lighting and sound operators to press their buttons for cue 53. The DSM also uses the radio relay to make sure the actors get to the right place backstage in time for their entrances and exits.

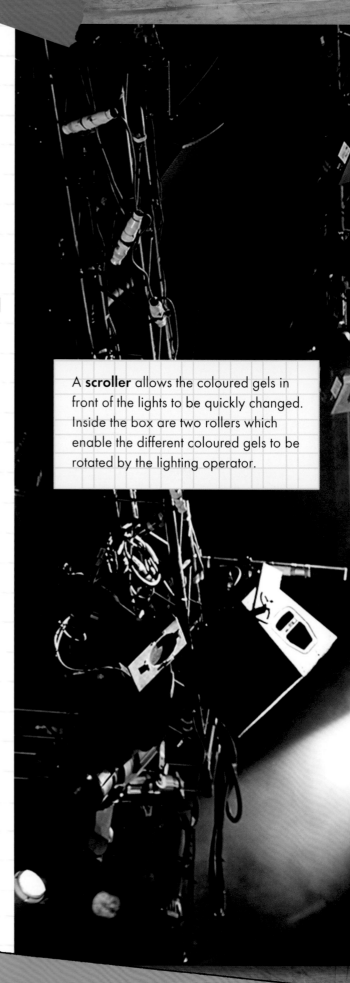

A **scroller** allows the coloured gels in front of the lights to be quickly changed. Inside the box are two rollers which enable the different coloured gels to be rotated by the lighting operator.

Lights known as **intelligent**, or **moving lights**, can be programmed and then controlled from the lighting desk, moving position and even changing their colour without anyone touching them. This one is a **moving profile light**.

Profile lights are used to shine a clearly defined spot of light on stage. They get their name from the fact they can be used to project the shape of anything placed between the light source and the lens. Shapes can be made by the light's shutters or by using a thin metal stencil, called a gobo.

Wash lights create a beam of light in a certain direction. Gels – thin films of plastic in different colours – are slotted in front of lights to make them change shade. Lenses can be used to change the shape of the light beam. This one is a **5kw Fresnel**, the brightest light you can use on stage.

Most theatre lights have tungsten light sources, as they are bright without being harsh. The operator can dim or black out (turn off) tungsten lights easily and quickly.

DIFFERENT TYPES OF LIGHT

This lighting rig shows four different types of light often found in theatres. Three other types of light are:

Floodlights, used for creating a wide splash of light on a backdrop or stage. The extent of the light can't be controlled.

Spotlights, used to follow an actor about on stage. They are often known as **follow spots**, and are useful if an actor is moving about a dark stage. They are moved by hand by a lighting operator, who has to keep up with the actor.

Some lights are fixed into place and focused on a particular spot on stage. They are called **generic lights**, and can be turned on and off from the lighting desk, but not moved.

THE CURIOUS INCIDENT OF THE DOG IN THE NIGHT-TIME

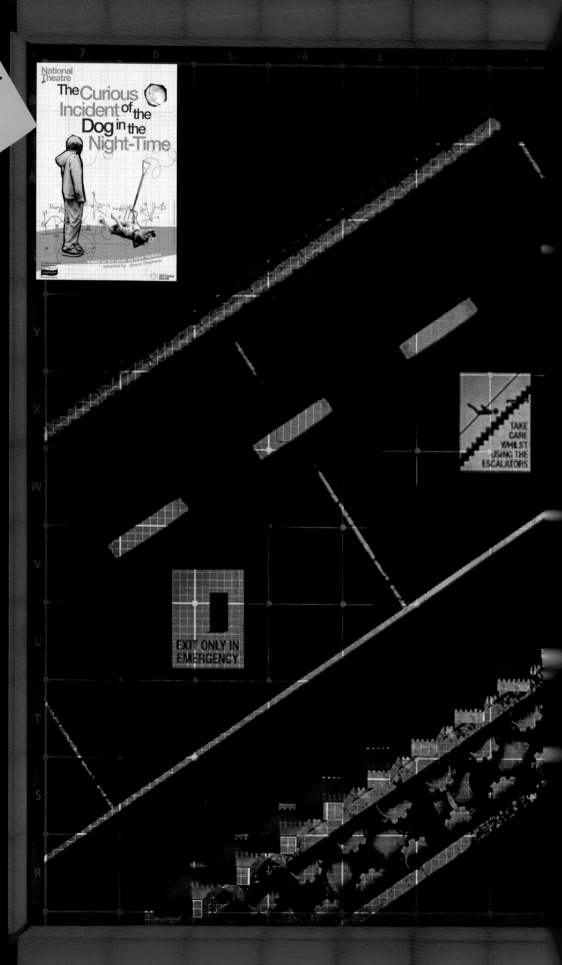

2012
Based on the novel by Mark Haddon
Adapted by Simon Stephens
Directed by Marianne Elliott
Designed by Bunny Christie

The Curious Incident of the Dog in the Night-Time is set in Swindon and London. The backdrop and stage look like a huge piece of graph paper. Outlines of houses, rooms and streets appear on the set floor and walls to create the illusion of these different places without any physical scenery being used. The scene can quickly shift by changing the lighting and video projection.

The lighting and video projection, designed by Paule Constable and Finn Ross respectively, also allows the audience to experience the intensity of Christopher's thought processes. He finds being in new places difficult, so when he takes a trip to London, fast-moving lights and huge words projected onto the walls and floor show how overwhelming he finds it.

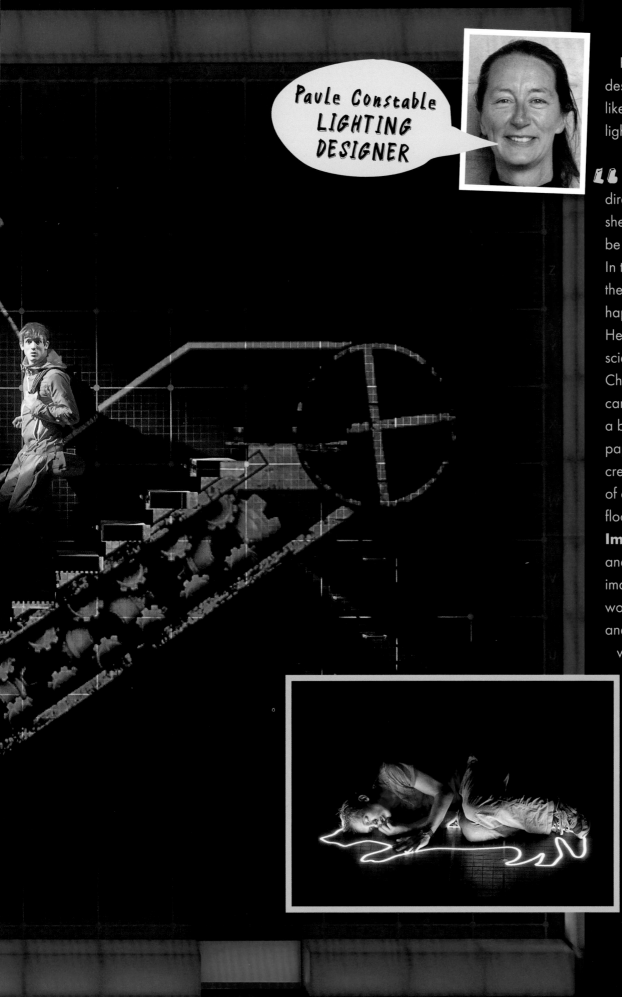

Here, Paule Constable describes what it was like coming up with the lighting design:

" Marianne Elliott, the director, made it clear she wanted the show to be driven by Christopher. In the book he describes the things that make him happy and unhappy. He likes computers and science and space. Bunny Christie, the designer, came up with the idea of a black piece of graph paper. We wanted to create a heightened sense of a grid, with pixels on the floor, almost like **Mission Impossible**, with dots and flashing lights. I imagined that Christopher would love the technology, and would want to see what the lights did and how they worked. We decided to draw the lines of the street using lighting and projection. Then we added the sound element, the noise of the street, which goes silent when he goes into a house. "

SOUND

SOUND

Sounds and sound effects create a
sense of place for the audience. When combined with a set,
costumes and lighting, the right sounds bring the play to life.

CREATING NOISE

Sounds play an important part in creating the play's world. You can buy sound effects, but sound designers also record their own when they are out and about and hear something good. Sometimes they go to great lengths to get just the right noise – even travelling to far-off countries. The sound designer will build the sounds, a bit like the way a musician will compose a score. The sound designer might create the sounds from scratch, remix or edit existing sounds and music, or work with live musicians to create sounds during the performance.

Some of the sounds you hear on stage are crucial to what's happening in the play, such as if a phone rings or the actors are listening to a radio. But sound designers also add sounds throughout the play that the audience won't really notice. These help to create the right atmosphere at different moments. If the play is set in a busy city, the distant noise of traffic might help set the scene. Strange noises can also create a sense of tension and change the mood or pace of the play.

Crumpling up crisp packets makes the noise of a fire.

Swirling dried peas around on a tray sounds like the sea.

SOUNDS ON STAGE

Speakers are positioned all around the stage to make the noises the audience hear as three-dimensional and believable as possible. If actors hear a sound coming from a television, there will often be a speaker hidden inside it to amplify the sound. Microphones can also be hidden inside props to amplify the volume when actors sing. Costumes can even be wired up to a tiny amplifier and speaker, which is useful if someone's phone has to ring in their pocket. It's the job of the sound operator, who sits in a control room at the back of the theatre, to connect all the speakers, make sure they are working and then control all the different sounds during the performance.

Bang a pair of gloves together to make the sound of wings flapping.

Pre-recorded sounds for
A SMALL FAMILY BUSINESS

Sound designers are very good listeners. They are alert to noises that most of us don't even notice, such as distant clocks ticking, or the rumbling of a fridge, or leaves rustling in the wind. Listen out for as many sounds as you can, not just the obvious ones. Where you are sitting right now, how many separate noises can you hear? Can you hear anything outside the windows? What about in the room around you? If you want to make your own sound effects during a performance there are several things you can do.

Jonathan Suffolk **HEAD OF SOUND AND VIDEO**

With sound, you're creating the rest of the world. It might be the sea outside a window, a road in the distance, or a train track. It puts you somewhere. It's a kind of geography.

Frozen lettuce makes the noise of flesh or bone being squished.

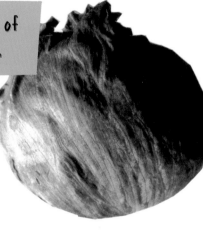

An old chair will make a creaking noise.

HOW they USED TO DO IT

In Shakespeare's time, cannonballs rolling over the theatre roof were used to create the sound of thunder. Theatres also used a device called a thunder run, which was a wooden trough on a pivot holding a cannonball that could roll back and forth. Later, thunder effects included shaking a sheet of metal.

Make a squelchy noise by rubbing soapy hands together.

Making sounds like these live during a performance is called a Foley technique. Foley was first used in radio broadcasting.

tricks of the trade

When actors wear microphones, speakers are needed to broadcast the sound. But the audience have to believe the noise is coming from the actors, not the speakers. One trick is to have a very slight delay on the sound from speakers at the back of the theatre. This is because sound does not travel as fast as light. With a delay, the real sound of the actor's voice arrives at the back of the theatre at the same time as it comes through the speakers, so there is no echo effect.

Adrian Sutton COMPOSER

A composer creates original music to help tell the story. The music must never draw attention to itself and the director always gets to say if a piece is right for the play. Music is a very powerful weapon for suggesting emotion or how an audience should react, so you have to use it carefully. It also has the power to put the play in different positions – like the geographical location or the mind of a particular character.

MUSIC

Music is very important to the sound of a play. It sets the mood and can tell you when and where the play takes place. Music can also smooth over a scene change or show the passing of time. Actors might also have to sing and dance during a play.

THE PERFECT TUNE

Sometimes theatres will hire a composer to write music for a play. Composers have to work quickly and talk to the director in advance about what is needed, as they don't have long to write the music. Using live musicians is useful as they can respond to what is happening on stage. If an actor is singing on stage and going faster than usual, it's no problem for the musicians to play faster. A band is also fun for the audience to watch. Music can also be recorded and played back during the performance.

Choosing the right instruments is important. A harpsichord tells the audience they are going back in time, while modern pop music shows it's the present day. In **War Horse** the actors sing songs by the folk musician John Tams, which poignantly sets the play in a now lost era. Different kinds of chord help set the mood. Major ones sound happy, minor ones sound sad and diminished chords are neither happy nor sad, and make the atmosphere spooky and uncertain.

MUSICALS

Not all theatres put on musicals, as they are a big challenge to create, rehearse and produce. But they can be very successful and popular. They normally have specially composed music and live musicians. Everyone in the cast has at least one microphone, and sometimes up to five. If the actor has to tap dance, they might have one microphone on each leg to amplify the noise of their feet. They might also have two microphones by their mouths, so there is a back-up in case one stops working.

TRY THIS AT HOME

If you want to make live music but don't have instruments, use whatever you can. Drumming on saucepans or blowing over the tops of glass bottles will create atmospheric music.

THE LIGHT PRINCESS

National Theatre

The **Light** Princess

a new musical
music and lyrics by **Tori Amos**
book and lyrics by **Samuel Adamson**

2013
Music and lyrics by Tori Amos
Book and lyrics by Samuel Adamson
Suggested by a story by George MacDonald
Directed by Marianne Elliott
Designed by Rae Smith

The Light Princess was a dark fairy-tale musical about a princess who had no gravity, so she floated, based on a story written by George MacDonald in 1864. Tori Amos and Samuel Adamson worked together extensively to write the music, story and lyrics. The story was told completely through singing and the production wove together choreography and aerial effects with dance, circus skills, puppetry and animation.

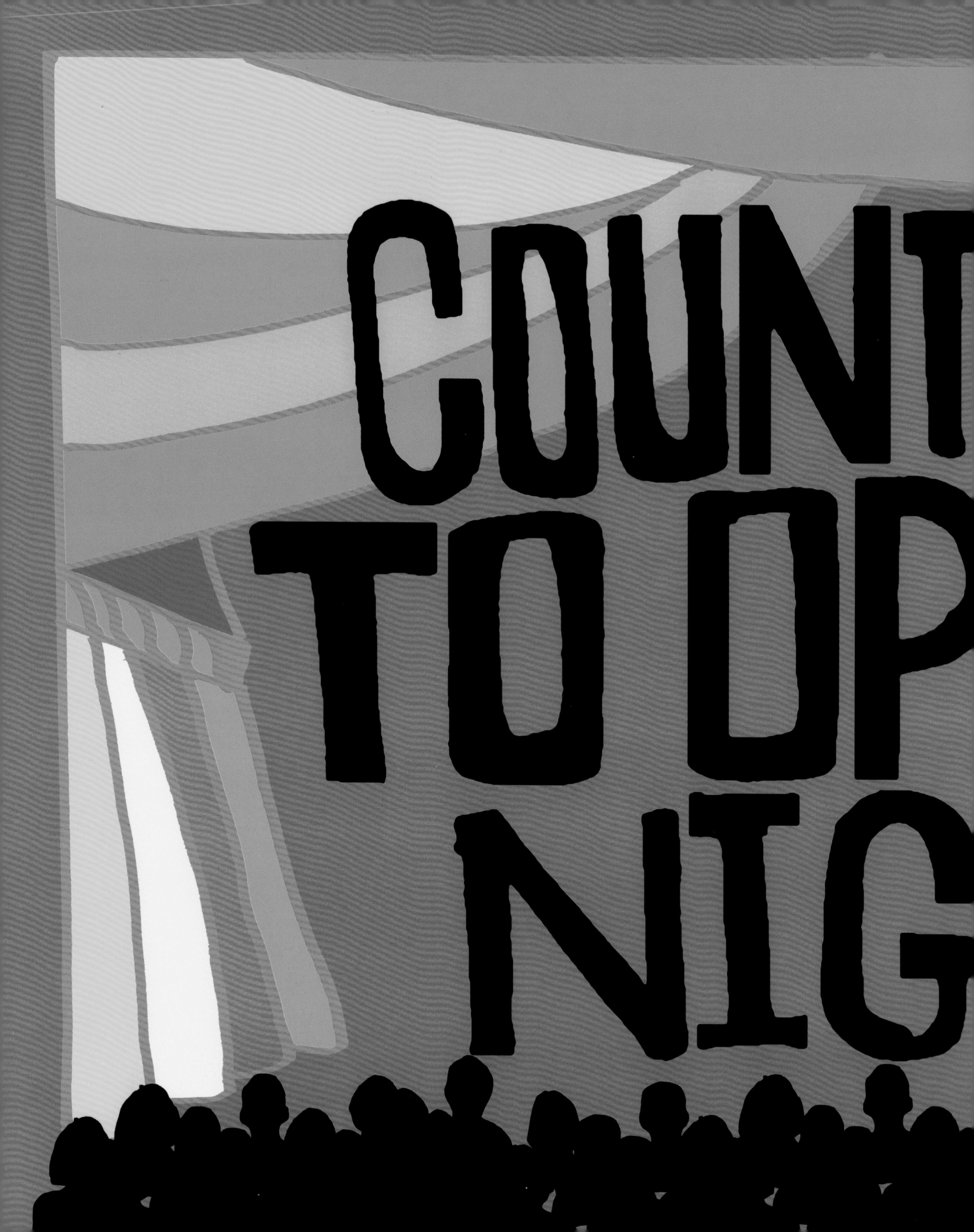
COUNT
TO OP
NIG

Posters, though effective and lovely to look at, are by no means the only form of communication. We now live in a digital age where people are viewing information about productions on their phones, for example.

THEATRE WORDS

A **MATINEE** performance of a play means the play is being performed in the afternoon. Sometimes theatres will have matinee and evening performances on the same day.

FINDING AN AUDIENCE

As soon as a play is chosen for the performance schedule, the theatre's marketing and press departments will start thinking about what sort of audience will like the play and how to reach them to tell them about it.

THE POSTER

Theatres use lots of different ways to market a play. Posters in public places like bus stops or train stations are a visually effective way of telling people about a play. The image on the poster will have been chosen to tell people something about the play instantly and also to convey the overall mood. The image will be discussed and agreed with the director. The National Theatre is famous for its posters.

As well as creating a great poster, theatres will email people who have been to see one of their plays before and tell them about new shows. They also make brochures. A theatre's website is also an important source of information, as are Twitter, Facebook and Instagram.

PRESS AND PUBLICITY

The theatre will make sure the play is featured in newspapers, magazines, websites and blogs and also on the radio and television. The actors or directors will give interviews and a photographer will take pictures of rehearsals and the performance to promote it.

NATIONAL THEATRE POSTERS

FRONT OF HOUSE

Before the audience take their seats for a performance they wait in the foyer, the area at the front of the theatre. Here there is the box office, where people can buy and collect their tickets, and a café or a bar serving snacks and drinks. If there is an interval, a short break normally in the middle of the performance, the audience will often leave their seats and come back to the foyer, where front-of-house staff will be on hand to sell programmes with information about the play and tell the audience more about the performance.

STATS & FACTS

THE NATIONAL THEATRE SELLS...

3,000 programmes every week.

More than 100,000 tubs of ice cream every year.

The most popular flavours are:

Chocolate: 20,376 tubs

Stem ginger: 19,656 tubs

Vanilla: 17,496 tubs

Caramel and hazelnut: 18,432 tubs

Strawberry: 10,584 tubs

Lemon sorbet: 8,616 tubs

TRY THIS AT HOME

Don't try to sum up the whole play on a poster. Try to evoke the right atmosphere instead. Start with a great image. It could be a picture of one of the actors in the play, or it could reflect the play's design, such as the set, or one of the costumes. Using bold colours can help your poster stand out, and a clear typeface will make sure everyone who sees it knows what they are looking at.

TREASURE ISLAND

Othello
by William Shakespeare

She Stoops to Conquer
by Oliver Goldsmith

National Theatre
MAN + SUPERMAN
by Bernard Shaw

National Theatre
Travelex £15
everyman
a new adaptation by Carol Ann Duffy

Cynthia Duberry
STAGE MANAGER

I really love running technical rehearsals. In rehearsals you are this lovely little unit – actors, director and stage management – and then you move into the theatre and your family becomes a lot bigger, because the rest of the design and creative team are there. You think, 'Now I can see what you're talking about. We've talked and talked about it for weeks and weeks, and now I can actually see what you meant.' Sometimes it can take three hours to tech twenty minutes of a play. I'll set a timetable out, and it might be twenty minutes for four minutes of play, because it's a really big sequence, but when you get through it you think, 'Wow, we've done it! And now we can move on.' We do a lot of scheduling, and it's a lot of guesswork: 'I think we can fit that in an hour.' It's like a jigsaw that you're constantly moving around. And it's great when your guesswork actually comes to fruition. It is lovely when it works.

BEFORE OPENING NIGHT

The set is built, the costumes and props are ready, the lighting and sound equipment is in place and the actors and director have rehearsed every scene and run through the whole play. In the technical and dress rehearsals all the different elements of the play and all the people involved have to work together to make everything ready for the first performance.

Technical rehearsals in the theatre

The Tech

For the technical rehearsal the actors leave the rehearsal room and move into the theatre for the first time. The tech is a slow run-through of the play, putting every technical cue into place: the sound effects, lighting changes and scene changes. It will be the first time the actors and the production team have worked together and it can take an agonizingly long time.

Plays at the National Theatre usually have three or four days of tech rehearsals, but sometimes they are the moment when big problems emerge, for example if the scene changes take too long. Actors and crew often dread the tech, but others love to see the show coming together. The stage manager is in charge of running the tech and making sure it proceeds on time, and they have a microphone to let everyone know what is happening.

THE DRESS REHEARSAL

If all goes to plan, the dress rehearsal is just like a performance, but without an audience. Everything should run just as it would in a normal show, and thanks to the tech rehearsal all the lighting and sound cues should now be working smoothly. Of course it isn't always like that, and if there are still any problems, now is the time to fix them. There's an old saying that a bad dress rehearsal means a good first performance, which can be a comforting thought if everything seems to be going wrong.

THE PREVIEWS

For a few performances before the official opening night, audiences can get cheaper tickets for previews. Depending on the production, these could be completely polished performances, or the director may still be making finishing touches. Some directors will be making big changes every night, for instance whole scenes could be scrapped if the play is running too long. Actors may also find their performances change in response to the audience's reaction during the previews. They can be very important for comedies as it's a way for the actors to find out what the audience will find funny and means they can adjust their timings accordingly.

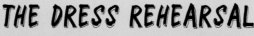

Olivia Vinall ACTOR

I think one of the most special but terrifying moments of my life was the first preview of **Othello**. There's nothing like the first time you have to go out there and perform it in front of an audience. I was so nervous that Rory Kinnear, who played Iago, practically had to push me on stage. I felt like I was going into a gladiator arena.

Paul Handley PRODUCTION MANAGER

I make sure that we achieve the ambition of the production within its budget. So that's lighting, sound, costume, props, wigs, all of that. I have to make sure that technically we're achieving the production's aims every night. It's about making something really solid that will work, night after night. The end of the process for me is the press night, the point when we've got the show as good as we think we can make it before showing it to the critics.

Tom Wicker
THEATRE CRITIC

A press night can be a glamorous affair, particularly if there are star names in the cast. I tend to skulk in a corner, trying to hide my notebook. And my goal is always to stay open-minded. No producer, director or actor actively sets out to do bad work. And in smaller venues, they are often working to a shoe-string budget, with very little (or no) pay. You can't like everything – and it's miserable when you don't – but I try to be fair and explain why. I don't see reviewing as an opportunity for target practice.

Meera Syal
ACTOR

Being written about is part of an actor's job and you have to develop a very thick skin. It's hard not to take it personally, but you have to remember whatever critics write is only their personal opinion, good or bad, and audiences will tell you much more about whether they are enjoying or not enjoying a play.

OPENING NIGHT

Opening night is also known as press night because it is when critics come to see the show. Actors know that and many get incredibly nervous about how their performances will be judged. They are likely to be full of adrenaline and may find themselves doing things on stage that they never did in rehearsals, which can be nerve-racking for the director to watch.

TRADITIONS AND SUPERSTITIONS

Actors can be superstitious, which isn't surprising as many things can go wrong on stage. There's a tradition at the National Theatre on opening nights. All the actors performing in the three different theatres will bang on the windows of the dressing room block, which face each other across a courtyard. This is their way of showing their support for the cast that is due to perform in their opening night.

COUNTDOWN TO A PERFORMANCE

Actors usually arrive at the theatre a few hours before the show begins. They do a physical and vocal warm up, apply their make-up and get into costume. They can use the stage until the auditorium opens and the audience are let in, about half an hour before the show begins.

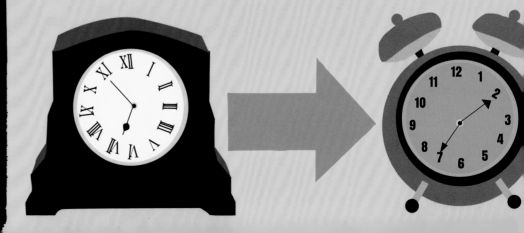

Actors never say good luck to each other before going on stage as it's meant to be unlucky. Instead they say "break a leg", ironically wishing each other one of the worst things that could happen on stage. They will also never say the name of Shakespeare's play **Macbeth** out loud, as it is supposed to be bad luck, so instead call it "The Scottish Play".

Paterson Joseph
ACTOR

WHEN THINGS GO WRONG

If an actor is suddenly taken ill and can't go on stage, big theatres will use an actor called an understudy to play the role instead. The understudy might already have a small role in the cast or be completely separate from the production. They have to learn all the lines, rehearse all the scenes, and have costumes and possibly wigs fitted, but they may end up never going on stage.

STAGE FRIGHT

Sometimes actors suddenly feel terrified of going on stage, even if they have done it hundreds of times before. It might last just a few seconds, but some actors have given up working in theatre altogether after a sudden attack of it.

THEATRE WORDS

When the audience really love a play, they stand up to clap at the end, which is known as a **STANDING OVATION**. It doesn't always happen, so when it does it is a very special feeling for the actors.

I had a tiny second of stage fright, which I've never suffered from before or since, when I was about to go on to fight in **Henry IV**. I was playing Hotspur and there was a big fight with me and Prince Hal at the end. It was a long sequence with a broadsword and shield. I thought, 'I'm about to go on, and I can't remember the first move. Is it a cut to the head? Do I lunge first?' A rush of panic came over me. I went on, and I stared at the other actor, and I'm sure he could see there was something wrong. But then he went for the first move and it was fine. It all came back.

Actors get warnings at set times so they know when the play will start. The deputy stage manager (DSM) will announce these over the backstage announcement system.

The 'half' is half an hour plus five minutes before the show starts, so 6.55pm for a 7.30pm performance.

The 'quarter' is a quarter of an hour plus five minutes, so 7.10pm.

The 'five' is five plus five minutes, so 7.20pm.

'Beginners' is five minutes before the show starts, so 7.25pm. That's when everyone in the opening scene needs to be ready. The DSM will say "Beginners please!" and formally list the names of the actors needed for the first act.

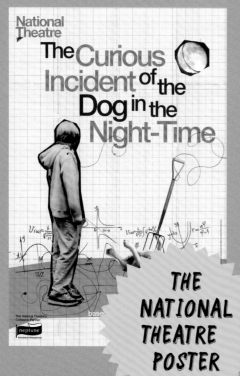

THE NATIONAL THEATRE POSTER

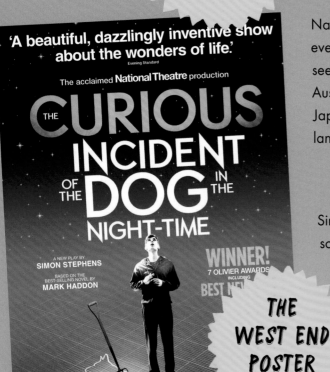

THE WEST END POSTER

AFTER THE FINAL CURTAIN

For some directors, the opening night marks the end of their work on the play. Other directors like to pop in and see it again every so often to make sure everything is still running the way they want it. Often it depends if they have already moved on to work on their next project. But sometimes a play can be so successful it will move to another theatre after its initial run so more people can come and see it.

THE WEST END

If a play at the National Theatre is a big success, sometimes its run will be extended, meaning it will come back for more performances. But if those performances are also selling out, it might be time to think about moving the play to a West End stage. Lots of National Theatre productions have gone on to have long runs in the West End, including **War Horse**, **One Man, Two Guvnors** and **The Curious Incident of the Dog in the Night-Time**. That way, audiences can still come and see them, but the National Theatre's stages are available to put on new shows, which may already have been planned.

ON TOUR

National Theatre shows also sometimes go on tour around the country – or even around the world. That means people who live far from London can see them. **War Horse** toured to theatres across the UK, the USA and Australia, as well as being performed in Canada, South Africa, Germany, Japan, Belgium and the Netherlands. It has also been translated into foreign languages like Mandarin, so audiences in China can enjoy the play.

NT LIVE

Since 2009, performances of plays at the National Theatre have been screened in cinemas across the country and around the world. Thousands of cinemas are now involved in the project. Most of the time, plays are shown live, though recorded performances are shown in cinemas in different time zones, such as in America and Australia.

IN FLANDERS FIELDS MUSEUM

WAR HORSE

2007
Based on a novel by Michael Morpurgo
Adapted by Nick Stafford
In association with Handspring Puppet Company
Directors Marianne Elliott and Tom Morris
Designer/Drawings Rae Smith

By May 2015, **War Horse** had been
seen by at least ...

2.6 million people in London
700,000 people in the rest of the UK
270,000 people in the Netherlands
710,000 people in New York
1.2 million people in the rest of the US
390,000 people in Canada
240,000 people in Australia
180,000 people in Berlin
140,000 people in South Africa
35,000 people in Japan
... and that's not including people who
saw it in cinemas with NT Live.

★★★★★
'An Entertainment Phenomenon.'

The acclaimed National Theatre production
WarHorse
warhorseonstage.com

Berlin · London · New York · Toronto · Melbourne
Das Theater-Ereignis des
Jahrzehnts kommt nach Berlin.
The National Theatre of Great Britain production · WarHorse
Gefährten
Ab Oktober in Berlin.

GETTING INVOLVED

There are lots of different ways to get involved in theatre and make plays. Here are just a few ideas.

For more fun ways to get involved in theatre go to nationaltheatre.org.uk/allabouttheatre

National Theatre Connections

Tim Hatley
DESIGNER

If you want to become a designer, start thinking about communicating visually. If you can't draw, try and learn. Go and see things. Take advantage of cheap tickets. Even if you think you're not going to like it, just go. Also know that you want to tell stories, and learn how to read and understand plays.

✻ Look out for theatre festivals like National Theatre Connections. It's a national festival of new plays for youth theatres and schools, and every year it introduces thousands of young people to new theatre skills.

✻ Go and see as many plays as you can at all different kinds of theatres. There are hundreds around the country so you are never that far away from one. If you can't go to the National Theatre, look out for its plays broadcast in cinemas through NT Live.

✻ Take part in drama at your school. If your school is putting on a play or musical, get involved as an actor, or ask if you can help out with the costumes, lighting or whatever interests you most backstage.

Behind the scenes at the National Theatre

Jessica Raine
ACTOR

I was quite shy as a child, but when I was about 13 I auditioned for **Bugsy Malone** at my school and got the part of Tallulah, which is such a great part. I remember that feeling of being on stage and loving it, and then after it finished I just wanted to do it again, and do it again better.

Bijan Sheibani
DIRECTOR

Going to see as much theatre as possible can help you decide what kind of theatre you want to make, and can introduce you to different practitioners. Writing to people whose work you like is a good idea, as this is how you begin to immerse yourself in the industry, and begin to develop relationships with people.

🎬 Go backstage. Lots of theatres will have backstage tours which show you behind the scenes. At the National Theatre there are backstage tours every day, where you can see different departments at work. You can also visit the Sherling High-Level Walkway, with views over the backstage workshops of the theatre.

🎬 Look out for drama groups in your local area. Your local theatre may run projects for young people or might be able to suggest a nearby group. These are great ways to meet other people who are also interested in the theatre.

🎬 Keep reading. Even if you can't see a play on stage, you will often be able to read the script. Your school or local library is a good place to look.

South Bank
London SE1

ational
ational

OTHELLO
Sun 26 May 2013 2.00 PM
latecomers may not be admitted

£15.00
STANDARD

Return code: 5

Order Number: 127777229

A 20

ON LEVEL 2

OLIVIER THEATRE

THEATRE WORDS

Acts are groups of scenes that form sections in a play.

The **auditorium** is the area of the theatre building where the seats and the stage are.

Body language is when an actor uses their movements or position to tell the play's story.

A **black out** is when the lights on stage are turned off.

Bringing the house down is a phrase used when the audience laugh or clap for a very long time.

A **call** is the time an actor must be ready for a certain moment.

Casting is when a director chooses actors to be in a play.

The **chorus** is a group of actors who comment on the play's action.

Conventions are devices repeated on stage which the audience can attach meaning to.

Corpsing is when an actor gets a fit of the giggles on stage.

Cues are signals for something to happen on stage.

Curtain calls are when the actors come back on stage at the end of the play to acknowledge the audience's applause.

Dialogue is when two or more characters talk to each other.

Dramatic irony is when the audience know what is going to happen but the characters don't.

An **ensemble** is when actors perform together as a group.

The **final curtain** is a phrase used to describe the end of a play.

Flashbacks are when part of the play's story is told by recreating a moment in the story's past.

The **flies** are the space above a stage where lighting and scenery hang out of sight of the audience.

The **fourth wall** is when actors imagine there is a wall separating the stage from the audience.

A **freeze frame** is when the actors freeze in a moment of action.

Genres are certain types of theatre.

The **gods** are the cheapest seats in the theatre, usually the highest

and furthest from the stage.

Hot seating is a rehearsal technique where actors learn more about their characters by being questioned in role.

The **house** is another word for a theatre's auditorium or audience.

Iambic pentameter is a rhythmic pattern of stressed and unstressed syllables used in verse.

Interpretations are the different choices made about staging and performing a play.

Mime is a theatre style where the play's story is told using only physical actions.

A **monologue** is a speech performed by only one actor.

A **narrative** is a storyline which runs throughout the play.

Physical theatre is when the play's story is told mainly through movement and action.

Projecting is when an actor expands their voice to fill the space.

Repertory theatre is when one venue has more than one play on at the same time, with different plays performed on different nights.

A **rig** is a structure for supporting and using anything that hangs over the stage, such as lighting or curtains.

A **role** is a part in a play.

The **script** is the written text of the play.

Sight lines are the different views the audience have of the stage.

A **soliloquy** is a solo speech performed by an actor which gives an insight into their thoughts.

Storyboarding is when a designer draws a picture of each scene to show how one turns into another.

The **subtext** is when the character is thinking differently to what they are saying.

Suspension of disbelief is when the audience believe what is happening in a play even though they know it isn't actually real.

Theatre practitioners are people who have a certain theory about theatre which informs their practical work, like Bertolt Brecht.

The **wings** are the left and right sides of a stage that are unseen by the audience.

PICTURE CREDITS